PLAYING THE GUITAR IN WORSHIP

The Lord is marching out (O give thanks)/Graham Kendrick/Copyright © Kingsway's Thankyou Music 1986.
Holiness unto the Lord/Danny Daniels/Copyright © Mercy Publishing/Kingsway's Thankyou Music 1989.
Here is Love/William Rees/Copyright © Scripture in Song/Kingsway's Thankyou Music 1978.
An army of ordinary people/Dave Bilbrough/Copyright © Kingsway's Thankyou Music 1983.
Be bold, be strong/Morris Chapman/Copyright © Word Music USA, (a division of Word Music (UK) Ltd) 1983.
Let us praise His name with dancing/Pale Sauni/Copyright © Scripture in Song/Kingsway's Thankyou Music 1983.
Hosanna/Carl Tuttle/Copyright © Mercy Publishing/Kingsway's Thankyou Music 1985.
Let Me have My way among you (Do not strive)/Graham Kendrick/Copyright © Kingsway's Thankyou Music 1977.
When I feel the touch/Keri Jones & David Matthew/Copyright © Springtide/Word Music (UK), (a division of Word Music (UK) Ltd) 1978.
I will seek Your face, O Lord/Noel & Tricia Richards/Copyright © Kingsway's Thankyou Music 1990.
River wash over me/Dougie Brown/Copyright © Kingsway's Thankyou Music 1980.
Seek ye first/Karen Lafferty/Copyright © Maranatha! Music USA. Word Music (UK), (a division of Word Music (UK) Ltd) 1972.
Ascribe greatness/Peter West, Mary Lou Locke & Mary Kirkbride/Copyright © Peter West Administered by Integrity's Music 1979.
Emmanuel/Bob McGee/Copyright © C.A. Music. Word Music (UK), (a division of Word Music (UK) Ltd) 1976.
Father God, I wonder (I will sing Your praises)/Ian Smale/Copyright © Glorie Music/Kingsway's Thankyou Music 1984.
I will sing of the mercies/J H Fillmore/Copyright © Kingsway's Thankyou Music 1991.
Holy is the Lord/Kelly Green/Copyright © Mercy Publishing/Kingsway's Thankyou Music 1982.
I just want to praise You/Arthur Tannous/Copyright © Acts Music/Kingsway's Thankyou Music 1984, 1987.
Jesus, how lovely You are/Dave Bolton/Copyright © Kingsway's Thankyou Music 1975.
Isn't He beautiful?/John Wimber/Copyright © Mercy Publishing/Kingsway's Thankyou Music 1980.
Worthy art Thou/Dave Richards/Copyright © Kingsway's Thankyou Music 1979.
Rejoice!/Graham Kendrick/Copyright © Kingsway's Thankyou Music 1983.
I love You, Lord/Laurie Klein/Copyright © House of Mercy Music/Maranatha! Music Word Music (UK) Ltd, (a division of Word Music (UK) Ltd) 1978.
I will call upon the Lord/Michael O'Shields/Copyright © Sound III Inc. Word Music (UK), (a division of Word (UK) Ltd) 1981.
Thank You, Jesus/Author unknown Arr. Margaret Evans/Arr. Copyright © Kingsway's Thankyou Music 1983.
Father, we love You/Donna Adkins/Copyright © Maranatha! Music, USA/Word Music (UK), (a division of Word (UK) Ltd) 1976, 1981.
I will sing unto the Lord/Donya Brockway/Copyright © His Eye/Cherry Blossom/Cherry Lane Music Ltd. Word Music (UK), (a division of Word (UK) Ltd) 1972.
Jesus, Name above all names/Naida Hearn/Copyright © Scripture in Song/Kingsway's Thankyou Music 1974/1979.
Open our eyes, Lord/Bob Cull/Copyright © Maranatha! Music USA. Word Music (UK), (a division of Word (UK) Ltd) 1976.
In my life, Lord (Lord, be glorified)/Bob Kilpatrick/Copyright © Bob Kilpatrick Music 1978.
For I'm building a people of power/Dave Richards/Copyright © Kingsway's Thankyou Music 1977.
He is Lord/Author unknown/Arr. Copyright © Kingsway's Thankyou Music.
When the Spirit of the Lord/Author unknown/Arr. Margaret Evans/Arr. Copyright © Kingsway's Thankyou Music 1983.

Addresses
Kingsway's Thankyou Music, PO Box 75, Eastbourne, East Sussex BN23 6NW, UK.
Word Music UK, (a division of Word UK), 9 Holdom Avenue, Bletchley, Milton Keynes MK1 1QR, UK.
Integrity's Music, PO Box 101, Eastbourne, East Sussex BN21 3UX, UK.
Bob Kilpatrick Music, PO Box 2383, Fair Oaks, CA 95628, USA.

Playing the Guitar in Worship

JOE KING

KINGSWAY PUBLICATIONS
EASTBOURNE

Copyright © Joe King 1995

The right of Joe King to be identified
as author of this work has been asserted by him in
accordance with the Copyright, Designs
and Patents Act 1988.

First published 1995

All rights reserved.
No part of this publication may be reproduced or
transmitted in any form or by any means, electronic
or mechanical, including photocopy, recording, or any
information storage and retrieval system, without
permission in writing from the publisher.

In the same series:
Playing the Keyboard in Worship by Stuart Townend

The songs referred to in this book can be found
in their entirety in *Songs of Fellowship* Music Edition
(ISBN 0 86065 935 6)

Copyright holders and addresses
are listed on page 2.

ISBN 0 85476 311 2

Designed and produced by
Bookprint Creative Services
P.O. Box 827, BN21 3YJ, England for
KINGSWAY PUBLICATIONS LTD
Lottbridge Drove, Eastbourne, E. Sussex, BN23 6NT.
Printed in Great Britain.

Contents

Part One – Strumming and Fingerpicking

1. The guitar: how to tune up; fingering; chords; the plectrum; the capo — 7
2. Strumming and fingerpicking: this book's method and how it works; the table of seven strumming patterns; key to the strumming patterns — 11
3. How to practise: the ten vital principles — 14
4. Strumming patterns: 1-7 — 19
5. Fingerpicking patterns: when to use fingerpicking; key to fingerpicking patterns; table of seven fingerpicking patterns — 34
6. Bar chords: basic types of bar chords — 38

Part Two – Enlarging Your Chord Vocabulary

7. Decorative chord work (1): using passing notes; using passing chords; chord combinations — 40
8. Decorative chord work (2): using bass note passing chords; how to use the passing chord tables; some easy examples; the bass note passing chord tables — 65
9. Chord sequences: when to use them — 73
10. Singing in tongues: guidelines for leaders; using the song melody; at the end of a song; out of a time of quiet — 76

Part Three – Leading Worship

11. The worship leader: as worshipper; as leader; body language — 82
12. The meeting: authority and accountability; do's and don'ts for leading worship — 87

Part Four – Creativity in Worship

13. Improving your worship: twenty-five ways to add variety — 93

Index of Songs and Pattern Numbers — 109

Acknowledgements

My thanks to Gerry Page for his helpful comments on the text and to Andrew Cleaton for reading the manuscript.

PART ONE

Strumming and Fingerpicking

1. *The Guitar*

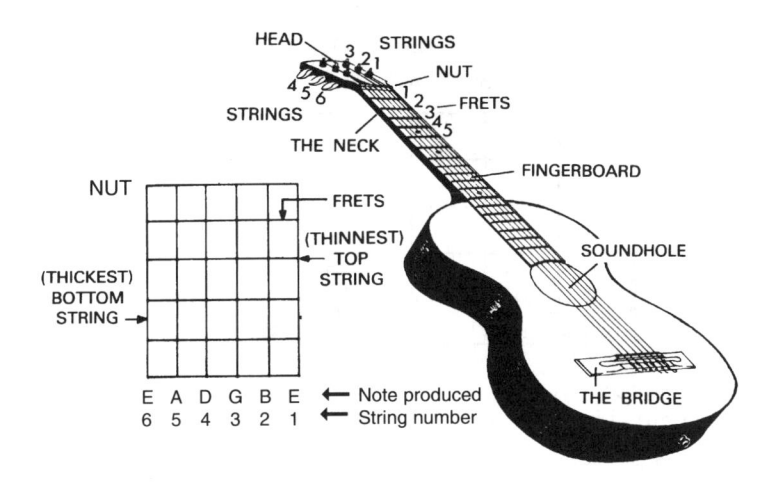

1. How to tune up

Apart from a tuning fork or pitch pipe, the quickest and most accurate method of tuning is with an electric tuner. Two tuners I would recommend are the Korg GT3 and Korg DT3 (which is twice as expensive as the GT3 but can be used to tune any instrument, not just the guitar). Important features on a tuner are (a) Automatic: This saves you having to flick a switch as you begin to tune each string; (b) Light indicator: Needles tend not to give as accurate a reading as a light indicator; (c) Bypass: If your guitar is amplified, then one lead can go from your guitar into the tuner and another from the tuner to the amplifier, so that if your guitar has been going out of tune during performance, you can quickly retune it between songs; (d) Facility for a power supply.

If you don't have a tuner, this is a procedure you could follow:

(a) Listen to the cassette* (example 1) and tune your 6th string to the note given there, which is an E.
(b) Count 5 spaces up the neck of the guitar, starting at the *nut* (which counts as 0). Place your finger firmly on the E string (6th) just behind the 5th fret. The note it gives you is the note to which the A string (5th) has to be tuned. See the diagram.
(c) Repeat this process with the A and D strings, then with the D and G strings.

---

* A cassette or CD is available to accompany this book. All examples are numbered and are included on both the cassette and the CD.

(d) In the case of the G and B strings, count 4 spaces up the neck along the G string, placing your finger firmly behind the 4th fret. The note it gives you is the note to which the B string has to be tuned.

(e) For the B and E strings, count 5 spaces up, placing your finger firmly behind the 5th fret on the B string. Tune your E string to this note.

Here is the process I've just explained, only in diagrammatic form:

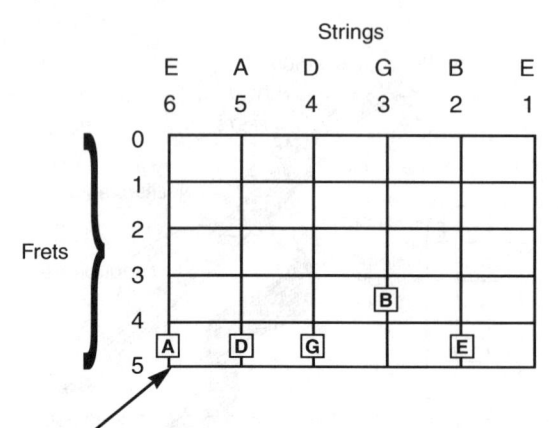

Place your finger here. The note it gives you (A) is the note which you tune the next string to. Repeat this process with each subsequent string.

If you are tuning your guitar to a piano, here are the notes to which you tune your guitar strings. Note: to make reading easier, music for the guitar is notated in the treble clef 𝄞, one octave higher than it actually sounds. (cassette example 2.)

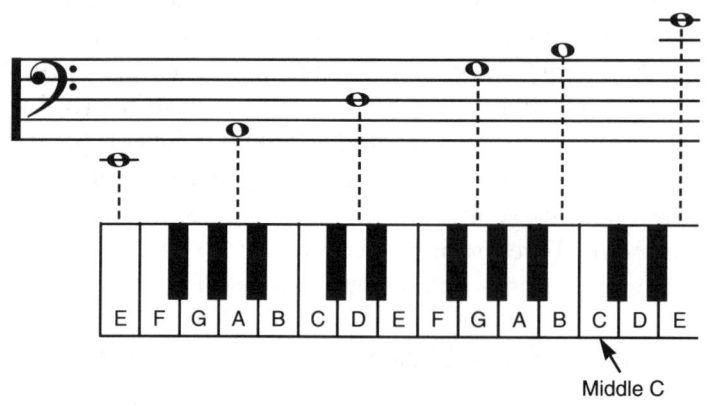

2. Fingering

Throughout this book (assuming that most guitarists strum and fingerpick with their right hand) fingers of the *left* hand will be marked 1 to 5, thumb to little finger, and fingers of the *right* hand T to 4, thumb to little finger.

3. Chords

Chord charts

All chords will be denoted like this:

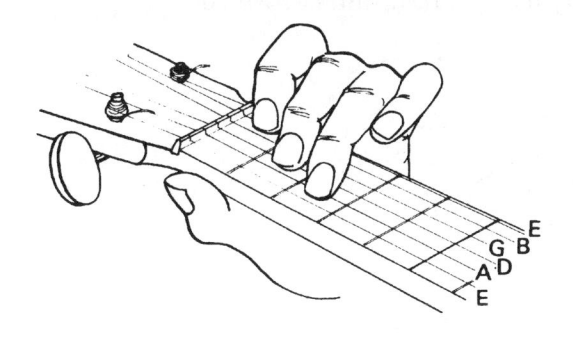

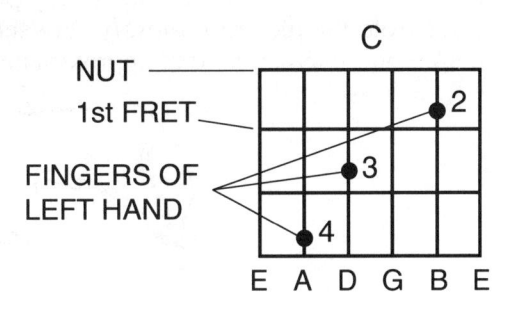

(Fig. 1)

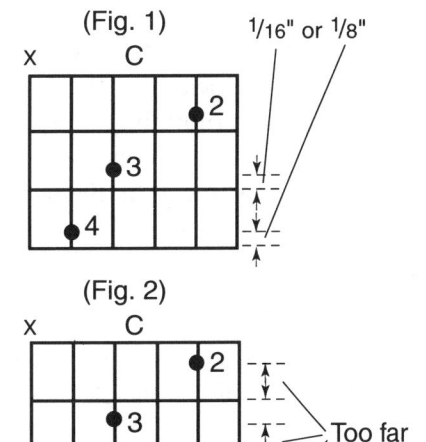

(Fig. 2)

(Fig. 3)

Placement of fingers

(a) If the fingers are much further away from the frets than is shown in Fig. 1 an unpleasant buzzing sound is likely to occur (Fig. 2).

(b) Make sure the wrist and the fingers are arched over the strings, or else one or two of the strings may be stopped from vibrating (Fig. 3).

(c) Use the *tips* of the fingers to produce a mellow tone.

(d) The small cross (x) at the top of a string means that that string is not to be played: it is not part of the chord. A string with no cross at the top is to be played open.

(e) Make sure the fingernails of your left hand are cut short or buzzing might result.

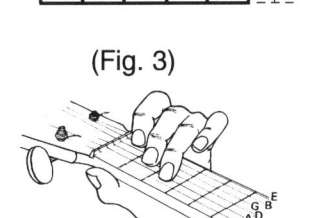

Pivot notes

You will notice in looking at the fingering for both Em and A7 that there is a finger common to both chords. The 3rd finger shouldn't leave its position as the hand swivels round ready for A7. This pivot note technique gives greater economy of movement. Look for it in other moves.

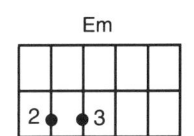

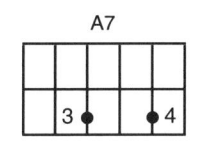

More advanced chords

If you see a chord which you don't know, you will probably find that it is playable by stripping it of all its 'additions,' eg Gmaj9, just play G; Dm9, just play Dm, etc.

4. The plectrum

I find the large, thin plectrums to my personal liking, but this may not be so in your case. Hold the plectrum *loosely* between the 1st and 2nd fingers on one side and the thumb on the other, so that approximately half the plectrum is covered.

Important note

The sign ▼ means 'accented stroke'. When the words and chords are given for a song this sign will appear over the words to indicate where the accents are to be played. The diagrams on strumming in each lesson will show more specifically where those accents come. The accents are not to be produced by strumming harder, but rather by a sharper movement of the wrist. Without them, your strumming is in danger of becoming monotonous.

5. The capo

What the capo is doing is effectively moving the 'nut' up the neck of the guitar. For every fret you move up, you raise the sound of the chord you play by one semitone. So, for example, if you play G on capo 1, you get A♭; if you play Em on capo 2, you get F#m.

Some songbooks give you a capo setting so that you can play easier chord shapes while remaining in tune with the piano.

'Capo 1' simply means that the capo is to be placed just behind the 1st fret. Here for example is the chord of G, capo 1:

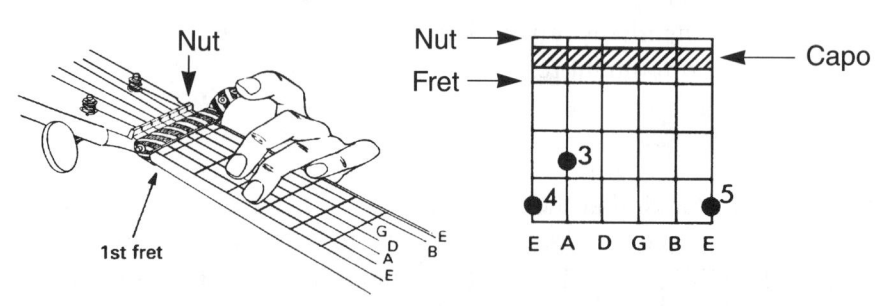

Piano keys (difficult for the guitar)	A♭	B♭	B	D♭	E♭	G♭
Guitar key	G	G	A	C	D	E
Capo placement	I	III	II	I	I	II

2. Strumming and Fingerpicking

This book's method and how it works

This is a proven method I have used in teaching over many years, but it is by no means universal.

When you come across a song and wonder how you should strum or fingerpick it, this method should help you.

Most songs fall into one of seven groups (styles), eg Ballad (slow), march (lively) and so on. Each of these groups has an underlying *pattern*. A pattern is a phrase repeated over and over.

Before practising a song, go through the following checklist and a quick process of elimination will lead you to the most appropriate pattern for the song.

(Cassette example 3 is a quick overview of the seven strumming and fingerpicking patterns.)

Pattern	time signature	Speed	Song example	S.o.F. no.	On-beat or off-beat songs	Other indicators to look out for
1	4/4	Lively	*The Lord is marching out*	536	1 + 2 + 3 + 4 + ▼ ▼ ▼ ▼	Hebrew style, Country style
2	4/4	Slow	*I give You all the honour*	210	1 + 2 + 3 + 4 + ▼ ▼	Ballads, meditative worship
3	3/4	Slow	*Abba, Father*	1	1 + 2 + 3 + ▼ ▼	Worshipful
4	6/8	Medium	*An army of ordinary people*	20	1+2+3+4+5+6+ ▼ ▼	Fast songs in 3/4 time
5	4/4	Lively	*Be bold*	37	1 + 2 + 3 + 4 + ▼ ▼	Songs with a dotted rhythm eg ♩. ♪
6	4/4	Lively	*I am a new creation*	197	1 + 2 + 3 + 4 + ▼ ▼	Celebration, rock
7	4/4	Lively	*Hosanna*	189	1 + 2 + 3 + 4 + ▼ ▼ ▼ ▼	Marches, hymns

An index of *Songs of Fellowship* songs with each song and its pattern number can be found at the back of this book.

If you learn the seven strumming/fingerpicking patterns, you should be able to play almost any song you come across, given also that you've mastered the chords for that song.

The patterns for both strumming and fingerpicking have been so arranged that strumming pattern 1 correlates to fingerpicking pattern 1 and so on. So when two guitarists are about to play a song, they should decide on an appropriate pattern, using the check-list above. Having done so, one can strum while the other fingerpicks. The resulting sound is more interesting than if both just strummed.

Note:
One song only is used to illustrate the same strumming and fingerpicking patterns. For example, *The Lord is marching out* is the song used for strumming pattern 1. Use this same song to practise fingerpicking pattern 1 too.

Key to the strumming patterns

↓	down-stroke
↑	up-stroke
▼	heavily accent that stroke (written as ▼ over the words of the songs)
—	strum the thicker 2/3 strings, starting from the bass note of the chord
---	strum the thinner 4/5 strings
～	strum all 6 strings on that stroke
②	(circled numbers) this is one of the main 'skeleton' strokes of the pattern
/	repeat
//.	repeat what was in the previous half of the bar
damp	Use the side of the right hand from the wrist to halfway up the little finger for this stroke (only used in pattern 5 and 6)

Time value of notes

♪	1/4 of a beat (or · which comes only in pattern 5)
♪	1/2 a beat
♪.	3/4 beat (this comes only in pattern 5)
↓	1 beat

The volume of each stroke

These go from 1 (very soft) to 10 (very loud)

▼	▼	▼	↓	↓	↑	↓	↑
～	～	---	～	—	～	---	---
DAMP							
10	9	9	6	6	6	4	1

very loud ―――――――――――――――――――― very soft

STRUMMING PATTERNS

SPEED	STYLE	TIME SIGNATURE	SONG EXAMPLE	PATTERN NUMBER	Beginner 1(a)	Intermediate 1(b)	Advanced 1(c)
Lively	Praise/Country	4/4	Ah, Lord God SoF 3	1			
Slow	Worship/ballad	4/4	I just want to praise You SoF 218	2			
Slow	Worship/ballad	3/4	Abba Father SoF 1	3			
Medium	Worship/praise/ballad	6/8	For this purpose SoF 114	4			
Lively	Praise/rock	4/4	Thank You, Jesus SoF 523	5			
Lively	Praise/rock	4/4	I am a new creation SoF 197	6			
Lively	Praise/march/Hebrew/hymn	4/4	I will build My church SoF 264	7			

Each pattern is split into three levels of ability, (a), (b) and (c)

The strumming pattern table explained

Each of the patterns 1 to 7 (5th vertical column in from the left) is subdivided into three levels of ability (top row). These are (a) beginner, (b) intermediate, and (c) advanced. This means that pattern 1(a), 1(b) and 1(c) are basically the same pattern. For example, a beginner could play pattern 1(a) while an advanced player would play 1(c) and they would find no clashing of down- or up-strokes. This is because the main accents are in the same place in both 1(a) and 1(c). This applies to all the patterns.
(Cassette example 4.)

3. *How to Practise*

Many people practise without any kind of method. When mistakes start cropping up they don't really overcome them, and over a lengthy period of time they end up actually practising mistakes. Bad habits become ingrained and difficult to remove.

Here are some ways of making economic use of your practice time.

1. Sectionalise the song

1st practice session – Introduction section only
2nd practice session – First half of the verse
3rd practice session – Second half of the verse
4th practice session – First half of the chorus
5th practice session – Second half of the chorus

Don't bite off more than you can chew in one session. You'll just end up with musical indigestion!

2. Practise individual chords

For each session of practice, look at each chord separately. Strum the first chord once and let it resonate. If the strings buzz or don't resonate clearly, check that your fingers are:
(a) Close to the frets ($1/16''$ is best).
(b) Arched (the index finger often catches the 1st string).
(c) Pressing the string hard onto the fret board.

3. Practise bass notes to chords

Each chord you play has a bass note. You should aim to pick this note out as you strum. The diagram, (Fig. 1) will help you to pinpoint where those bass notes are for each chord.

How to use the diagram

Example: Finding the correct bass note on the guitar for the chord of B7.
(i) Find which string (vertical lines) the letter name of the chord is on, in this case, the letter 'B'. It's on the 5th string.
(ii) Position your fingers on the fretboard for the chord of B7 (Fig. 2).

(iii) Strum your plectrum across the strings, making sure that the *first* string it touches is the 5th string.

You have now played B7 with the correct bass note of B.

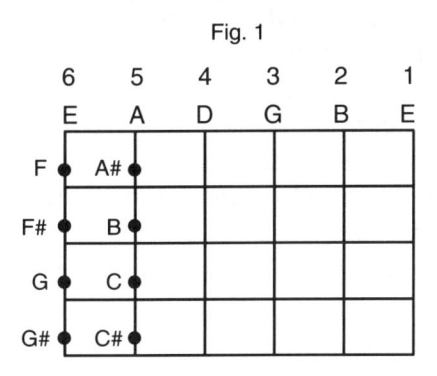

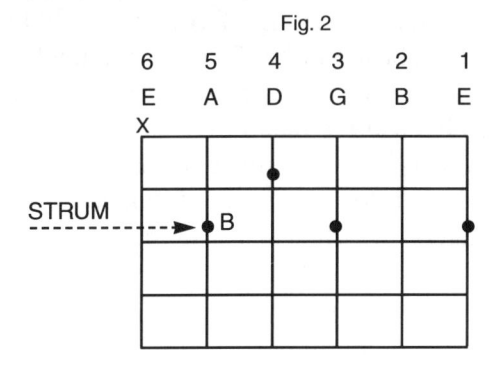

```
          Fig. 1                                    Fig. 2
  6   5   4   3   2   1              6   5   4   3   2   1
  E   A   D   G   B   E              E   A   D   G   B   E
                                     X
F●   A#●                                         ●       ●
                                   STRUM - - - → ●B      ●       ●
F#●   B●                                 
                                                 
G●    C●                                         
                                                 
G#●  C#●                                         
```

Note:
If you are in a key with flats, eg A♭ major, then F#, G#, A# and C# would become G♭, A♭, B♭ and D♭ respectively.

Chords such as B7 must be played with the correct bass note because if you accidentally hit the 6th string (E) a dissonance will result. This also applies for chords such as D.

4. Practise chord changes (Cassette example 5)

Quickly make a list of the various changes there are in the song. Don't repeat any. Now, use just one down-stroke for each chord. Don't introduce a strumming pattern yet. It will only confuse matters.

The following exercise is designed to help you to change chords quickly, using Am to G as an example. Look at this diagram and the points following it:

			simultaneously	
(i)	(ii)	(iii)	(iv)	(v)
count	strum	look ahead	move to next chord	strum next chord
1 2 3 4	1 2 3 4			1 2 3 4
	Am			G
(Bar 1)	(Bar 2)			(Bar 3)

(i) Count 4 beats in. They must be evenly timed. Keep even time throughout the exercise.
(ii) Strum the first chord firmly (Am) so that all the strings resonate clearly for 4 beats.
(iii) As soon as you've strummed the first chord (Am) *look ahead* to the next chord (G)

and to which fingers are to be used and where they are to be placed. Try to get (ii) and (iii) to happen almost simultaneously.
(iv) Don't take your fingers off the fretboard until *after* beat 4, otherwise the strings will stop resonating. If you do, you'll have a gap between the chords.
(v) Just as beat 1 of bar 3 comes in, quickly yet smoothly place your fingers onto the fretboard for the next chord (G) and at the same time strum the strings firmly, again ensuring that *all* the strings are sounding clearly.
(vi) Now try the same move *without* looking at the fingers of your left hand. This will help you to play by *touch* rather than by sight. It will also show up the weaker fingers, which will be strengthened by this exercise. When you get the move wrong, look at the fingers, repeating the exercise correctly. Then once more, repeat it without looking.

When you've got the first chord change moving smoothly, move onto the next chord change in the first section.

5. Practise strumming

Use only one chord so that you can concentrate on the strumming.
(a) *Only play the main down-strokes at first (▼ and ↓).*
These are the strokes usually with circled numbers and/or crosses above them, eg ① ⊕.
    (i) Look at the signs ——, ----- and ∿. This enables you to see on which strings these main strokes are to be played.
    (ii) Hold your plectrum loosely. These main accents are *not* produced by holding the plectrum too tightly. They come as a result of a sharp action from a loose wrist.
    (iii) Start at a speed which is comfortably slow for you. Keep that speed *regular*, no matter how slow.
    (iv) Play the first chord with these main strokes for about thirty seconds or until an even, rocking motion has been established. These strokes are the main 'pillars' which hold the rest of the pattern firmly in place. Unless these strokes are clearly pounding away in every bar, providing a clear pulse in the ear of the listener, when the up-strokes are introduced, the shape of the pattern will become vague and untidy.
    (v) Pay due notice to the numbers under the different strokes ($\underset{6}{\downarrow}$). These numbers show the volume at which strokes are to be played, on a scale of 1 to 10, 1 meaning 'very soft' and 10 meaning 'very loud'. They are only a guideline. Do not become over-focused on this, as it will lead to your playing sounding rigid.
        To make your overall playing sound even, make sure the volume of the strokes in one bar is repeated at the same volume in each subsequent bar.
(b) *Now add any further down-strokes (↓).*
Only when you've been able to produce an even, rocking motion with the main

down-strokes (marked either ↓ or ⇣) should you add the other less important down-strokes (marked ⇣).

(c) *Now add the quieter up-strokes (↑).*
   (i) As you do this, consistently maintain the volume of the main strokes. Strumming is given character by a contrast of accented and light strokes. As you introduce the up-strokes, make sure they are *extremely quiet*, otherwise the pattern will become cluttered. Holding the plectrum as loosely as possible will help you in this respect.
   (ii) There is a tendency when starting to strum to be timid in your approach. Keep a free action in your wrist and a fairly large arc as you strum. The smaller the arc, the more timid and tense you are likely to sound.

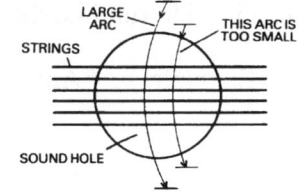

Summing up

(i)   Contrast accented strokes and very light strokes – produces interesting strumming.
(ii) Hold the plectrum loosely – produces light strumming.
(iii) A sharp action from a relaxed wrist – produces accents.
(iv) Practise slowly at first – produces controlled playing.
(v)   Use a large arc – produces freer playing.

6. Practise strumming while changing chords

Example: Pattern 1(c)

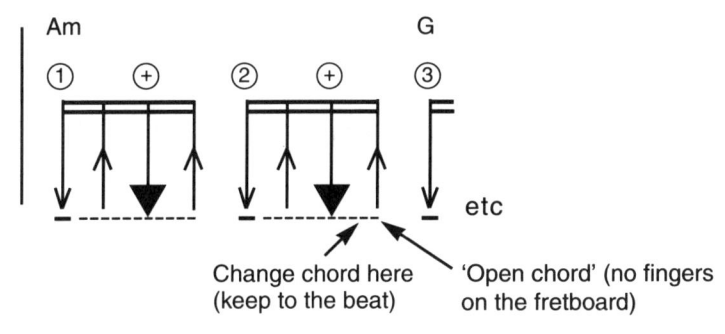

Change chord here (keep to the beat)   'Open chord' (no fingers on the fretboard)

(a) Start slowly

Count time evenly.

(b) Keep to the beat as you change chords

When strumming, resist the temptation to hesitate and lose time as you change from one chord to another. Continual faltering while changing chords can turn into a habit that is difficult to correct. It may help if you reduce speed so that you can change without faltering.

(c) Use the 'open chord' idea

See the diagram above. This term means that on the stroke indicated, no fingers are touching the strings. They have momentarily left the fingerboard on their way to a new chord.

(d) Connect the ringing of each chord

As you change, don't accidently stop the strings from resonating. Allow the ringing of one chord to run into the next chord.

```
Example:    Am (ring)   --------------------> G
            Strum                         no gap
            
            | 1      2       3       4  | 1
```

7. Practise the section marked $<$

The sign $<$ means 'increase volume'. This is best done by playing just down-strokes on the beats or words marked ▼.

After playing a phrase marked $<$ to bring about the increase of volume, it can be quite hard to resume the normal pattern; so isolate those parts of the song and practise like this:

(i) Pattern   (ii) $<$ (iii) Resume pattern

When you have gone through points 1 to 7 for the *introduction* of a song, repeat this process for the *verse* (dividing it into two sections) and the *chorus* (also dividing it into two manageable chunks).

8. Don't waste time

Don't be tempted to keep playing sections of the song you can do well when there are still parts of the song you're struggling with.

9. Revising

When returning to look at a passage you previously thought you'd got right, always start practising *slowly*. If you start playing it at performance speed, you're likely to make a number of slips and jump to the conclusion – wrongly – that you didn't practise properly the last time. Your confidence might become eroded and you will end up disillusioned at your lack of progress.

10. Little and often

It is better to have a number of short intense sessions of practice, rather than lengthier periods when concentration is likely to be less sharp.

4. *Strumming Patterns*

STRUMMING PATTERN 1

This pattern (Cassette example 6) is used for lively, praise, 4/4 time, 'country feel', Jewish style songs. (Songs with a Jewish flavour can also be played with pattern 7.)

Below are alternative diagrams for the pattern. Choose the version which you think suits your standard of playing. They are essentially the same pattern.

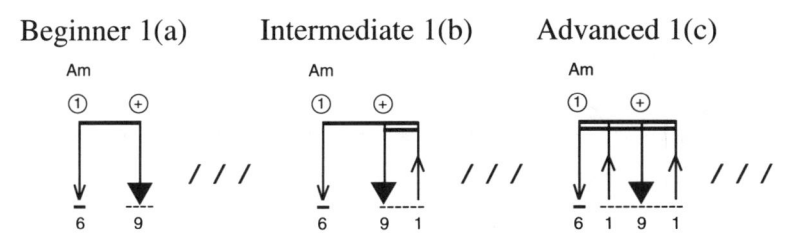

Beginner 1(a)   Intermediate 1(b)   Advanced 1(c)

Key

Numbers ringed, eg ① ⊕, are the main accents of the pattern
── means play the 2/3 strings at the bass end of the chord
----- means play the thinner strings
↓ means down-stroke
▼ means heavily accent that stroke

Time value of strokes

If you find the diagrams above difficult to understand, the following should help you to see how many strokes make up each beat:

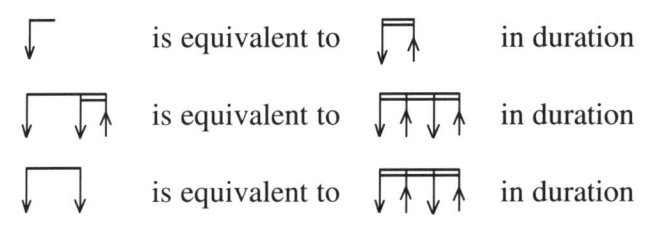

Summary (Cassette example 7)

(a) The main strokes are on beats ① and ⊕. Any other strokes, especially up-strokes, should be *very quiet* in comparison to these main strokes, otherwise your playing will sound over-busy.
(b) Hold the plectrum loosely. Keep your wrist relaxed.

(c) Accents are produced by a quicker action from a loose wrist, not by suddenly holding the plectrum tighter.

(d) Listen to your playing. Are any strings buzzing or not sounding? Eliminate this problem by keeping your fingers (i) close to the frets (ii) arched and (iii) pressed hard onto the fretboard.

Example: *The Lord is marching out (SoF 536)* (Cassette example 8)

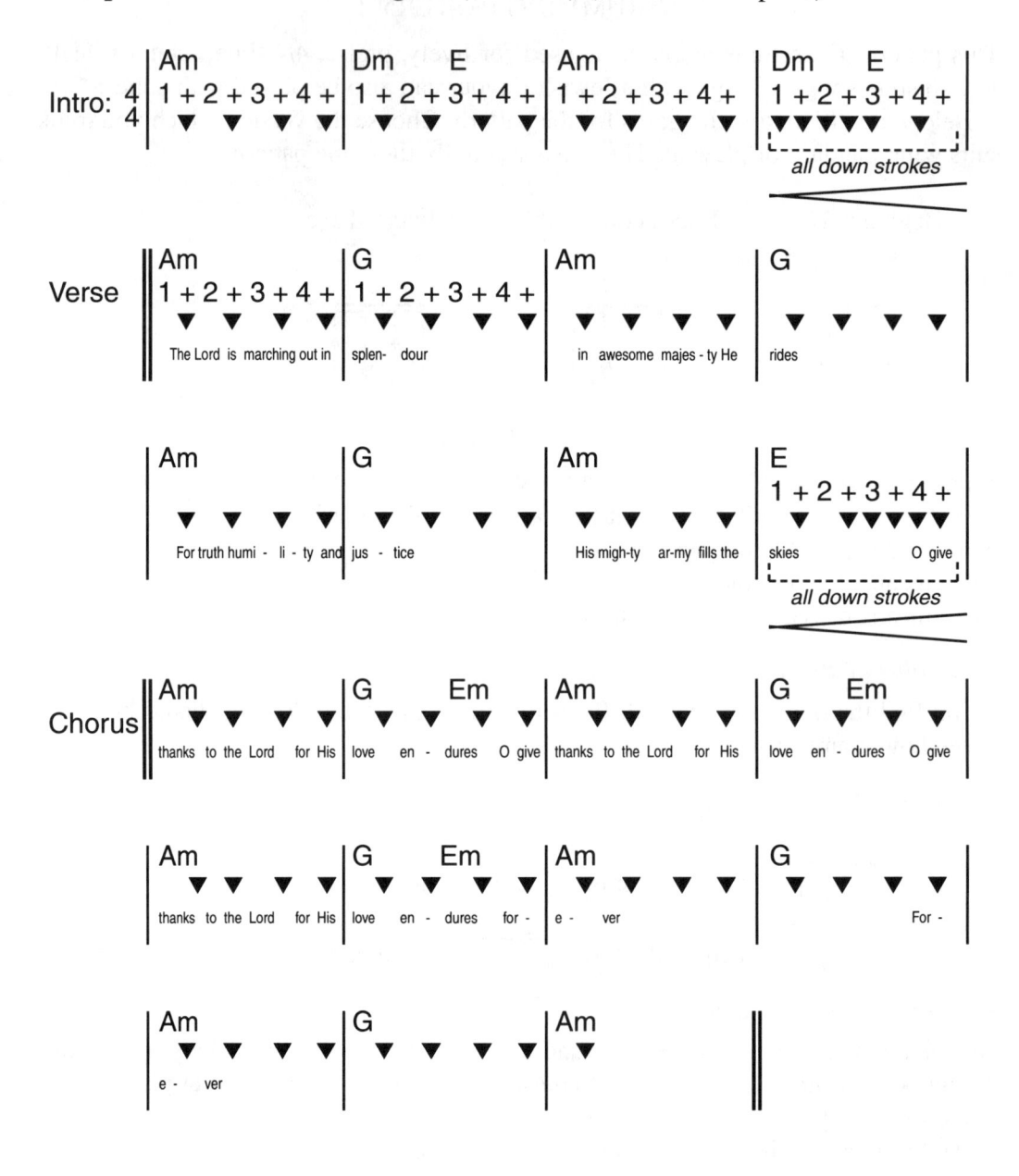

Intro: 4/4 | Am 1 + 2 + 3 + 4 + ▼ ▼ ▼ ▼ | Dm E 1 + 2 + 3 + 4 + ▼ ▼ ▼ ▼ | Am 1 + 2 + 3 + 4 + ▼ ▼ ▼ ▼ | Dm E 1 + 2 + 3 + 4 + ▼▼▼▼▼ ▼ |

all down strokes

Verse || Am 1 + 2 + 3 + 4 + ▼ ▼ ▼ ▼ The Lord is marching out in | G 1 + 2 + 3 + 4 + ▼ ▼ ▼ ▼ splen- dour | Am ▼ ▼ ▼ ▼ in awesome majes - ty He | G ▼ ▼ ▼ ▼ rides |

| Am ▼ ▼ ▼ ▼ For truth humi - li - ty and | G ▼ ▼ ▼ ▼ jus - tice | Am ▼ ▼ ▼ ▼ His migh-ty ar-my fills the | E 1 + 2 + 3 + 4 + ▼ ▼▼▼▼ skies   O give |

all down strokes

Chorus || Am ▼ ▼ ▼ ▼ thanks to the Lord for His | G   Em ▼ ▼ ▼ ▼ love en - dures O give | Am ▼ ▼ ▼ ▼ thanks to the Lord for His | G   Em ▼ ▼ ▼ ▼ love en - dures O give |

| Am ▼ ▼ ▼ ▼ thanks to the Lord for His | G   Em ▼ ▼ ▼ ▼ love en - dures for - | Am ▼ ▼ ▼ ▼ e - ver | G ▼ ▼ ▼ ▼ For - |

| Am ▼ ▼ ▼ ▼ e - ver | G ▼ ▼ ▼ ▼ | Am ▼ ||

Chords for this song

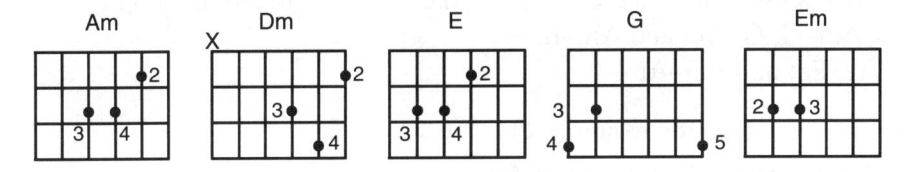

Am   Dm   E   G   Em

Bass notes for chords in this song (Cassette example 9)

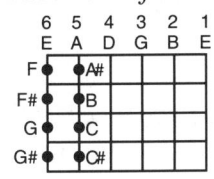

The bass note for the chord of A is the note A. The note A is on the 5th string, played open (without any fingers on it). In this and in future equivalent sections, the bass note for a chord will be notated thus: Am(5).

So the bass notes for the chords in this song are as follows: Am(5), Dm(4), E(6), G(6) and Em(6).

Here and in future song examples, whenever the sign $<$ is used, it is an instruction to increase volume by playing just down-strokes. It helps to break up the repetition of the pattern. After you've practised these phrases, make sure you practise how to get back into the pattern, so that the main strokes are as evident as before.

Principles of practice

As you begin to practise this song and the other songs in this book, make sure you follow the vital principles of how to practise, in Chapter 3. Let's see how they apply.

● *Sectionalise the song*

First, practise the *introduction* using principles 1 to 10, then practise the *verse* using the same principles, and lastly the *chorus*.

● *Practise individual chords*

The chords for this song are Am, Dm, E, G and Em.

● *Practise bass notes to the chords*

Here's an example:
(a) Place your fingers on the fretboard for the first chord, Am.
(b) Strum the strings, making sure that the first string you touch is the 5th string. You have now played Am with the correct bass note of A.
(c) Here are the other chords in the song with the string you should strum first so that you play the correct bass note: Dm(4), E(6), G(6) and Em(6).

● *Practise chord changes* (Cassette example 10)

Strum from the bass note of each chord. Each time you come to a song, quickly make

a list of the various changes, not repeating any. For this first song they are:
Introduction: Am–Dm, Dm–E and E–Am (get these correct before moving on).
Verse: Am–G, G–Am and Am–E.
Chorus: G–Em and Em–Am.

● *Practise strumming* (Cassette example 11)

Use only *one* chord. For this first song use Am.
(a) Only play the main down-strokes at first.
   (i) Look at the signs ▬, ▬▬ and ﹏.
       These tell you on which strings these
       main strokes are to be played; in this case ↓ ▼.
   (ii) Hold the plectrum *loosely*, not tightly. Remember, accents are produced with a sharp action from a loose wrist, not from holding the plectrum any more tightly.
   (iii) Start at a speed which is comfortably slow for you. Keep that speed *regular*, no matter how slow.
   (iv) Play Am with the two main strokes ↓ ▼.
       Keep repeating this until an even rocking motion has been established.
   (v) Take note of the volume of each stroke (numbers under the strokes).
(b) Now add any other down-strokes.
(c) Now add the quieter up-strokes.
   (i) As you do this, keep the volume of the main strokes *loud*.
   (ii) Keep a free action in your wrist and a *large arc*.

● *Practise strumming while changing chords* (Cassette example 12)

Always strum from the bass note of a chord.
(a) Start *slowly* and count time *evenly*.
(b) Keep to the beat as you change chords.
(c) Use the open-chord idea.
(d) Connect the ringing of each chord. Avoid gaps appearing.
(e) Don't allow the pattern to become uneven. Concentrate on the main strokes.

● *Practise the sections marked* ⟨ (Cassette example 13)

(i) Dm–E   (ii) E

Then practise resuming the normal pattern (particularly the main strokes).

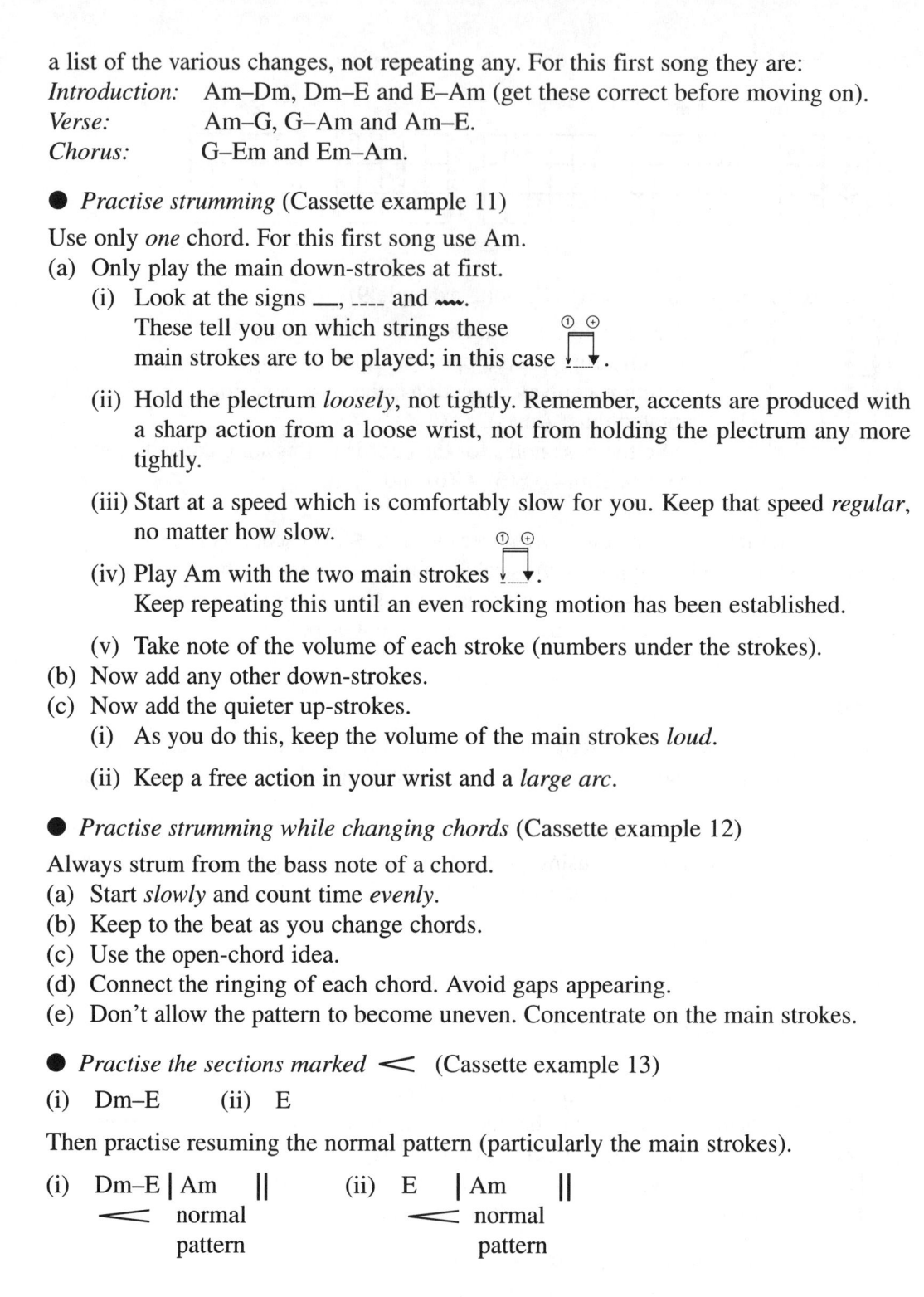

(i) Dm–E | Am   ‖   (ii) E | Am   ‖
     ⟨   normal   ⟨   normal
         pattern   pattern

Final note

- The main stroke(s) should always stand out clearly above the others.
- As the pattern is repeated, make sure the main stroke(s) maintain the same volume.
- As you practise a new pattern, start with the main stroke(s) and only when these are secure should you add the other strokes.
- If the addition of these other strokes causes your playing to become uneven, revert to playing just the main strokes and begin the process once more.

STRUMMING PATTERN 2

This pattern (Cassette example 14) is used for slow, worship, 4/4 time, medium-paced hymns and songs.

Below is the pattern graded in three levels of ability.

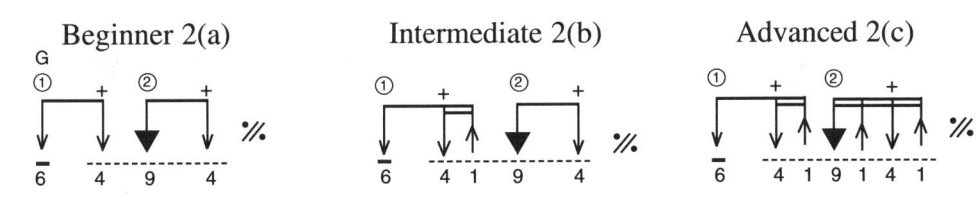

| Beginner 2(a) | Intermediate 2(b) | Advanced 2(c) |

Key

See page 22

Time value of strokes

See page 22.

Summary (Cassette example 15)

(a) Make the stroke on beat ② much louder than all the others. ① is the next loudest.

(b) There should be a rocking motion created between beats ① and ②.

(c) All strokes apart from those on beats ① and ② should be very quiet, especially the up-strokes.

(d) Start by just playing the main strokes on beats ① and ②. As you are able to repeat bar after bar evenly, only then add the other strokes. If you sense you are losing the evenness, revert to playing just the two main strokes and start the process again.

(e) Hold the plectrum loosely. Keep your right wrist relaxed, especially on accented strokes.

Example: *Holiness unto the Lord (SoF 180)* (Cassette example 16)

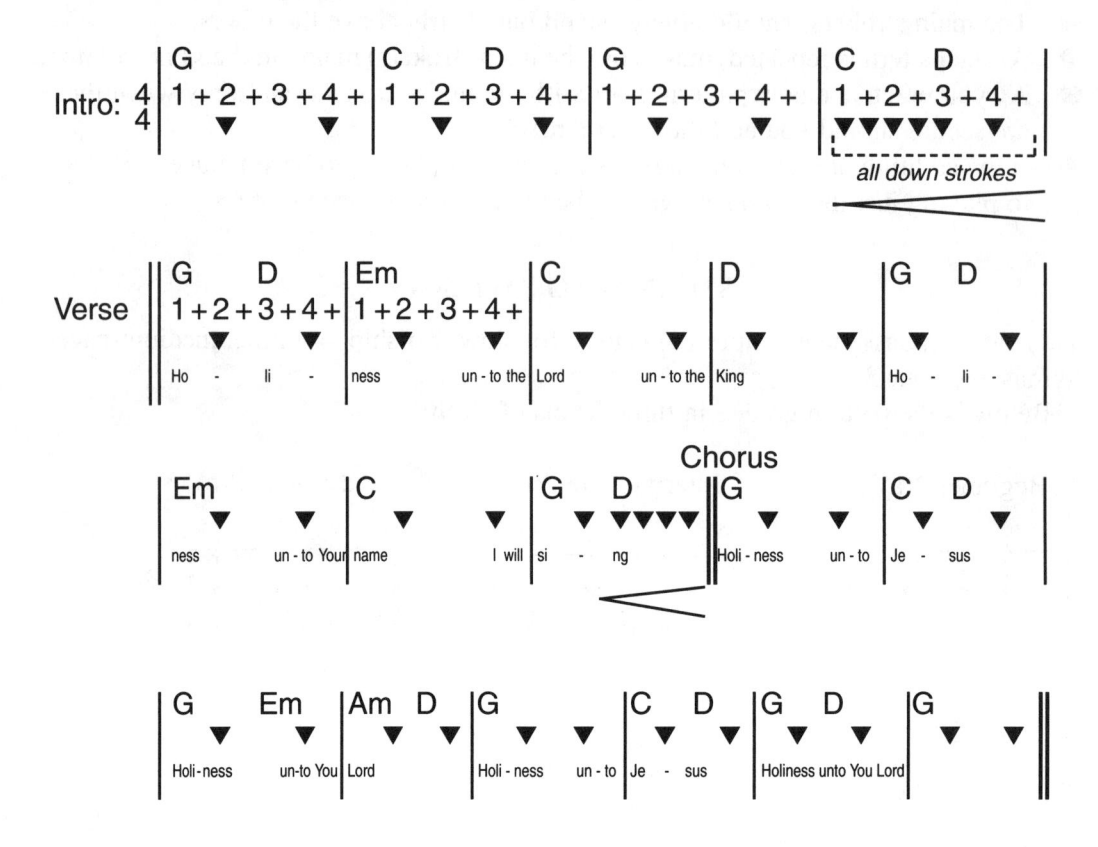

Intro: 4/4 | G 1+2+3+4+ ▼ ▼ | C D 1+2+3+4+ ▼ ▼ | G 1+2+3+4+ ▼ ▼ | C D 1+2+3+4+ ▼▼▼▼ ▼ |

all down strokes

Verse ‖ G D 1+2+3+4+ ▼ ▼ | Em 1+2+3+4+ ▼ ▼ | C ▼ ▼ | D ▼ ▼ | G D ▼ ▼ |
Ho - li - ness un - to the Lord un - to the King Ho - li -

| Em ▼ ▼ | C ▼ ▼ | G D ▼ ▼▼▼▼ | **Chorus** ‖ G ▼ ▼ | C D ▼ ▼ |
ness un - to Your name I will si - ng Holi - ness un - to Je - sus

| G Em ▼ ▼ | Am D ▼ ▼ | G ▼ ▼ | C D ▼ ▼ | G D ▼ ▼ | G ▼ ▼ ‖
Holi-ness un-to You Lord Holi - ness un - to Je - sus Holiness unto You Lord

Chords for this song

G, Em and Am have already been covered, so the new chords are:

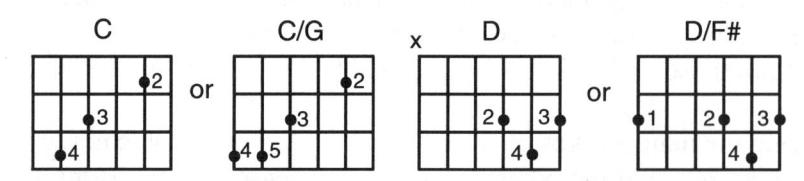

C   C/G   x D   D/F#

The chords C/G and D/F# are for advanced players. They are simply fuller sounding chords.

Bass notes for chords in this song (Cassette example 17)

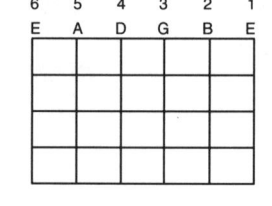

6 5 4 3 2 1
E A D G B E

C(5) or C/G(6), D(4) or D/F#(6)

Note: Remember, the numbers in brackets refer to strings.

Practise chord changes (Cassette example 18)

Certainly when first learning the guitar, make a list of the chord changes in the song. Don't bother to repeat changes that occur in other sections of the song. So for this song, the changes are:

Introduction: G–C, C–D, D–G
Verse: G–D, D–Em, Em–C, C–G
Chorus: G–Em, Em–Am, Am–D

Remember, while changing chords:
(a) Strum from the bass note of each chord.
(b) Set a slow beat and keep to that beat as you change chords.
(c) As you change, try to keep the strings resonating. Avoid the strings going 'dead' as you change. Make the change as late in the bar as possible.
(d) Don't allow the pattern to become uneven. Bring out the main strokes.
(e) Practise one section at a time. Get that section correct before moving on.

STRUMMING PATTERN 3

This pattern (Cassette example 19) is used for slow, worship, 3/4 time songs.
  Here are the alternative patterns:

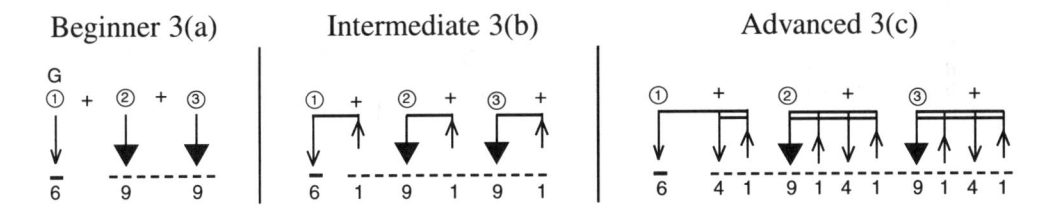

Beginner 3(a)   Intermediate 3(b)   Advanced 3(c)

Key
See page 22.

Time value of strokes

In addition to the time values illustrated in pattern 1, you now need to observe the following:

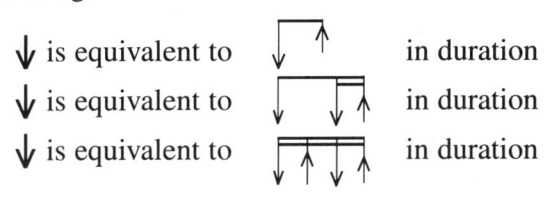

↓ is equivalent to ↓↑ in duration
↓ is equivalent to ↓↓↑ in duration
↓ is equivalent to ↓↑↓↑ in duration

Summary (Cassette example 20)

(a) Only play the main strokes at first (on beats ①, ② and ③) until the pattern is firmly established.

25

(b) The strokes on beats ② and ③ should be at similar volumes. The stroke on beat ① should be a little quieter.

(c) The strokes on beats ② and ③ should be played with a relaxed wrist. They should be played quickly. Avoid playing too deliberately, as the resulting effect can end up as slow, spread chords.

Example: *Here is love (SoF 168)* (Cassette example 21)

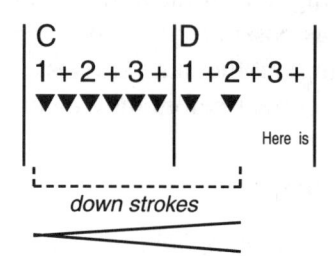

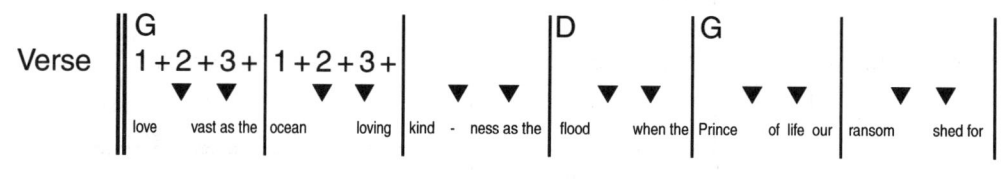

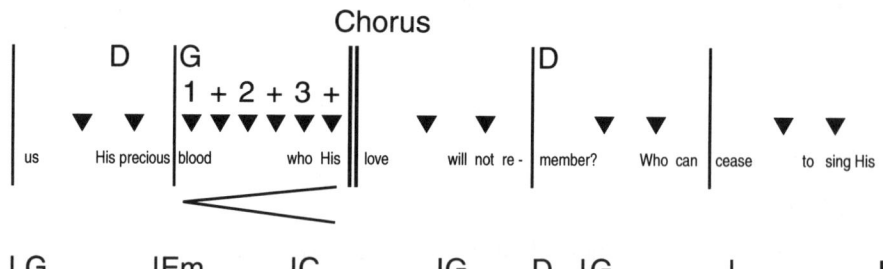

Intro: 3/4 | G 1+2+3+ | 1+2+3+ | C 1+2+3+ | D 1+2+3+ | G 1+2+3+ | 1+2+3+ |

| C 1+2+3+ | D 1+2+3+ |
down strokes

Here is

Verse: | G 1+2+3+ | 1+2+3+ | | D | G | | |
love vast as the ocean loving kind - ness as the flood when the Prince of life our ransom shed for

Chorus

| D | G 1+2+3+ | | D | | |
us His precious blood who His love will not re- member? Who can cease to sing His

| G | Em | C | G D | G | |
praise? He can ne - ver be for- gotten throughout heaven's eternal days

Practise

All the chords, bass notes and chord changes for this song have been covered in the previous patterns and songs. Even so, repeat the procedure we've been trying to establish for your times of practice.

(a) Chord changes

Introduction: G–C, C–D, D–G.

Verse: G–D.
Chorus: G–Em, Em–C, C–G.

(b) Remember, while changing chords:
(i) Set up a slow, even count.
(ii) Execute each of the moves in (a), trying to keep all the strings vibrating as you move.
(iii) The accents on beats ② and ③ should be the same volume and should be much louder than the other strokes.
(iv) The volume of each stroke in one bar should be exactly the same in each subsequent bar.

STRUMMING PATTERN 4

This pattern (Cassette example 22) is used for slow/medium, worship/praise, 6/8 time, or fast 3/4 songs.

Here is the pattern in three varying degrees of ability:

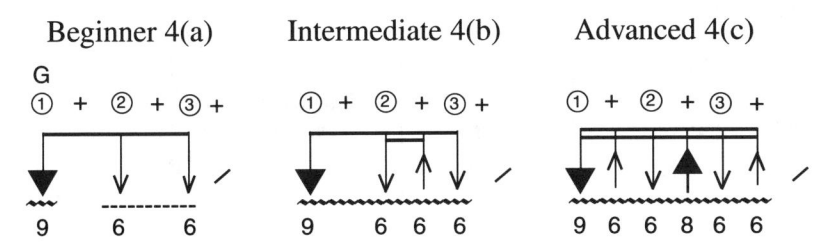

Beginner 4(a)   Intermediate 4(b)   Advanced 4(c)

G
① + ② + ③ +   ① + ② + ③ +   ① + ② + ③ +

9 6 6   9 6 6 6   9 6 6 8 6 6

Key

〜 means strum ALL the strings.
/ means repeat what has gone before.

Time value of strokes

If you are having difficulty understanding the pattern diagrams, the following should help:

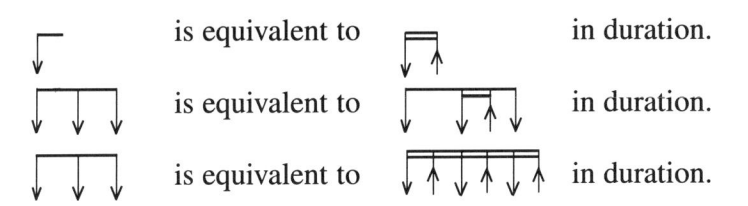

⌐ is equivalent to ⌐⌐ in duration.

⌐⌐⌐ is equivalent to ⌐ ⌐⌐ in duration.

⌐⌐⌐ is equivalent to ⌐⌐⌐⌐⌐⌐ in duration.

Because the sign 〜 is an instruction to strum *all* the strings where possible, the technique of picking out the bass note to each chord is not that vital. This is also true of patterns 5, 6 and 7.

Example: *An army of ordinary people (SoF 20)* (Cassette example 23)

Intro: 6/8
| **G** 1+2+3+4+5+6+ ▼ ▼ | **C** **D** 1+2+3+4+5+6+ ▼ ▼ | **G** 1+2+3+4+5+6+ ▼ ▼ | **C** **D** 1+2+3+4+5+6+ ▼ ▼ ▼ ▼ An |

Verse
| **G** **C** 1+2+3+4+5+6+ ▼ ▼ ar - my of or - di - nary | **G** ▼ ▼ people, | **Em** ▼ ▼ a kingdom where love is the | **C** ▼ ▼ key, | **Am** ▼ ▼ a city, a light to the | **G** ▼ ▼ nations, |

| **C** ▼ ▼ heirs of the promise are | **D** ▼ ▼ we. A | **G** **C** ▼ ▼ people whose life is in | **G** ▼ ▼ Jesus, a | **Em** ▼ ▼ nation together we | **C** ▼ stand. |

Chorus
| **Am** ▼ ▼ Only through grace are we | **G** ▼ ▼ worthy, | **C** **D** ▼ ▼ in - heri - tors of the | **G** 1+2+3+4+5+6+ ▼ ▼ ▼ ▼ ▼ land. A new day is | **C** ▼ ▼ dawning, |

| **D** ▼ ▼ a new age to | **G** ▼ ▼ come, | **Em** ▼ ▼ when the children of | **C** **D** ▼ ▼ promise | **D** ▼ shall flow together as | **G** 1+2+3+4+5+6+ ▼ ▼ ▼ ▼ ▼ one: – a truth long ne - |

| **C** **D** ▼ ▼ -glected, but the time has now | **G** ▼ ▼ come | **Em** ▼ ▼ when the children of | **C** ▼ ▼ promise | **D** ▼ shall flow together as |

| **G** ▼ ▼ one. | ▼ |

Practise

Constantly refer to chapter 3 on the vital principles of how to practise. If you implement these for each new song it will cut your practice time down to half. It will also mean that your playing will be of a higher standard than if you had no disciplined approach.

Don't keep playing the sections you can do easily and avoiding the bits which give you trouble. Your times of practice should primarily be focused on the problem areas.

Listen to your playing. Eliminate buzzing. Check that each string is resonating clearly. If you're not keeping a close ear to what sound you're producing, hidden bad habits can develop. Take time, and build slowly at first.

Constantly refer to the cassette which accompanies this book to hear the type of sound you should be aiming to produce.

STRUMMING PATTERN 5

This pattern (Cassette example 24), having a 'triplet' feel to it, is used for lively, praise, 4/4 time songs.

Here is the pattern in three levels of ability:

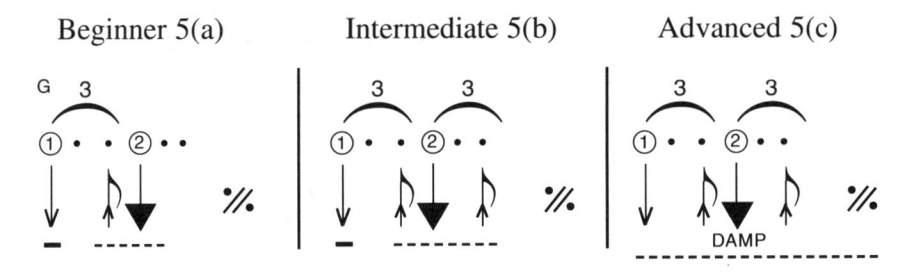

Beginner 5(a)   Intermediate 5(b)   Advanced 5(c)

Key

%. means repeat what was in the previous half of the bar.
〰 means play all the strings on the strokes marked 〰.
3   means 'triplet' (for an explanation see below)

Time value of strokes

In this pattern, a crotchet (one beat = ♩) instead of being divided into quavers (half-beats = ♪) or semi-quavers (quarter-beats = ♬), is divided into *three* beats. If the three beats are played they are noted thus: ♬³. If two beats are played then the notation is ♩³♪ or ♪³♩

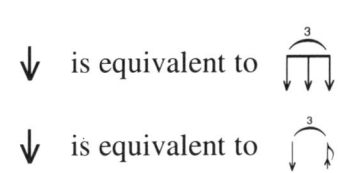

↓ is equivalent to ♬³

↓ is equivalent to ♩³♪

Example: *Be bold, be strong (capo 5) (SoF 37)* (Cassette example 25)

Intro: | G 1 2 3 4 | C 1 2 D 3 4 | G 1 2 3 4 | C 1 2 D 3 4 Be bold, |

Verse: | G 1 2 3 4 be strong, | For the | C Lord your God is with | D you. Be bold, | G be strong, |

| For the | C Lord your God is with | D you. | **Chorus** C D I am not afraid | Em | C D I am not dismayed |

| Em because I'm | C D walking in faith and | Em victory; come on and | C D walk in faith and | Em victory for the |

| C Lord your | D God is | wi - th | G you. ||

Damping (Cassette example 26)

(a) This is done by momentarily stopping the strings from vibrating *after* the 2nd stroke and *on* the 3rd. Listen to the cassette to hear the sound you are aiming for.

(b) The length of the arc of the stroke responsible for the damping remains the same as the other strokes.

(c) Even more 'bite' can be produced if you strum further up the strings than usual, on the section of the fretboard beside the sound hole.

(d) The side of the hand from the wrist to half way up the little finger is used for damping.

(e) Keep the hand very still as you execute the whole of this movement.

(f) The 'damp' is essentially brought about through a downward movement of the hand, *not* an inward movement towards the strings.

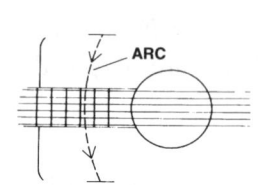

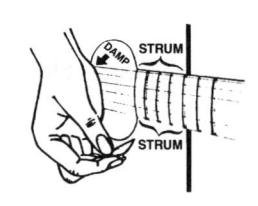

Practise

The method of practice for each song should largely be the same, varying slightly depending on the chords and pattern used. Here's a quick recap.

1. Practise a section at a time.
2. Play chords from the bass note up. Check all the strings are ringing.
3. If you're practising strumming, use only one chord so that you can concentrate on getting the pattern even.
4. When you're concentrating on getting chord changes smooth, don't be strumming with a pattern. Simply play one down-stroke on each chord.
5. Hold the plectrum loosely. Keep your wrist relaxed.
6. Play the main accent(s) of the pattern first until the general 'feel' of the pattern is emerging. Then add the other strokes. Make sure these additional strokes are quieter, otherwise the strumming will become cluttered.
7. Listen to your playing. Eliminate buzzing and other unpleasant sounds by keeping the fingers of your left hand (a) close to the frets, (b) arched so that you're playing on your fingertips, and (c) pressed down onto the fretboard.

Note: Keep the fingernails of your left hand short.

STRUMMING PATTERN 6

This pattern (Cassette example 27) is used for lively, praise, 4/4 time songs, and some hymns having a straight beat ♩♩.

Here is the pattern split into three levels of ability:

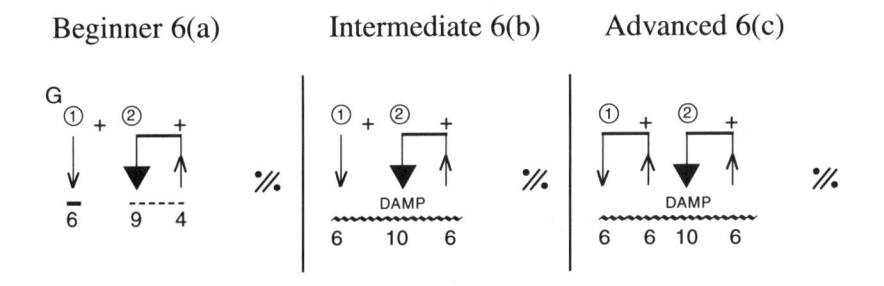

Beginner 6(a)   Intermediate 6(b)   Advanced 6(c)

Key

See page 22

Time value of strokes

See this section in pattern 3.

Example: *Let us praise His name with dancing (SoF 332)* (Cassette example 28)

Intro: 4/4 | G 1 + 2 + 3 + 4 + ▼ ▼ | C D 1 + 2 + 3 + 4 + ▼ ▼ | G 1 + 2 + 3 + 4 + ▼ ▼ | C D 1 + 2 + 3 + 4 + ▼ ▼ ▼ *down strokes* Let us |

Verse || G C 1 + 2 + 3 + 4 + ▼ ▼ praise His name with dan- | G 1 + 2 + 3 + 4 + ▼ ▼ cing   and | D ▼ ▼ with the tam-bou-rine | G ▼ ▼ Let us |

| G C ▼ ▼ praise His name with dan- | G ▼ ▼ cing | D ▼ ▼ make a joy-ful noise and sing. | G G⁷ ▼ ▼ |

Chorus | C ▼ ▼ Dance, | G ▼ ▼ dance, | D ▼ ▼ dance before the king. | G G⁷ ▼ ▼ | C ▼ ▼ Dance, |

| G ▼ ▼ dance, | D ▼ ▼ dance before the King. | G ▼ ▼ ▼ | ||

STRUMMING PATTERN 7

This pattern (Cassette example 29) is used for lively, praise, 4/4 time marches, Jewish style songs and hymns (although songs with a Jewish flavour can also be played with pattern 1 if you want an off-beat feel).

Here is the song in varying degrees of ability:

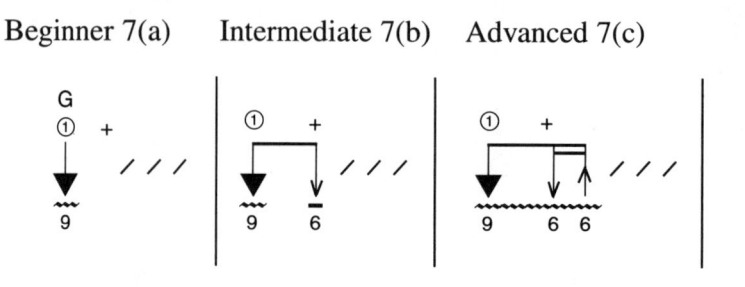

Beginner 7(a)   Intermediate 7(b)   Advanced 7(c)

Key
See page 22

Time values of strokes
See this section in pattern 3.

Example: *Hosanna (SoF 189)* (Cassette example 30)

5. *Fingerpicking Patterns*

When should you fingerpick as opposed to strumming?
1. When it's appropriate to the song. In the context of worship, this usually means quieter, more contemplative songs which use patterns 2, 3 or 4.
2. To create a different musical texture. The seven fingerpicking patterns in the following table correlate to the seven strumming patterns we've been looking at. Therefore, one guitarist could play a song such as *Ah, Lord God* which uses strumming pattern 1 and another guitarist could fingerpick pattern 1 and the two would fit together.
3. To add variety. You can mix strumming and fingerpicking in the same song by the following method. (Cassette example 31)

   Let's say you want to play the third verse of a song with fingerpicking and verses 1, 2 and 4 with strumming.

END OF VERSE 2   VERSE 3
(using strumming pattern 2)   (Fingerpicking pattern 2)

C	D		G								
1	2	3	4	1	2	3	4	1	2	3	4	etc

- The last chord at the end of verse 2 (strummed).
- The plectrum is flicked backwards into the cup of the hand and held there by the little finger and third finger.
- The fingerpicking is carried out by the thumb, index and middle fingers.

Key

T = The thumb of the hand which will be picking the strings.
1 = Index finger,   2 = middle finger,   3 = 3rd finger.
(2) = Finger 2 is an optional extra. The brackets ( ) round any finger number mean that it is not essential to include that note. It is only there to add more interest.
(2)/T = Pluck at the same time.
① = Accent with your index finger. (The circle sign means 'extra emphasis'.)
/ = Repeat.
∕∕. = Repeat the previous half of the bar.
♪ (triplet) = Triplet. (This only occurs in pattern 5. It means that the beat on which the triplet occurs is divided into three parts.)
①/Ⓣ = Pluck at the same time but also accent both fingers.

34

How this book's fingerpicking method works (Cassette example 32)

Example: Pattern 2 on the chord of E

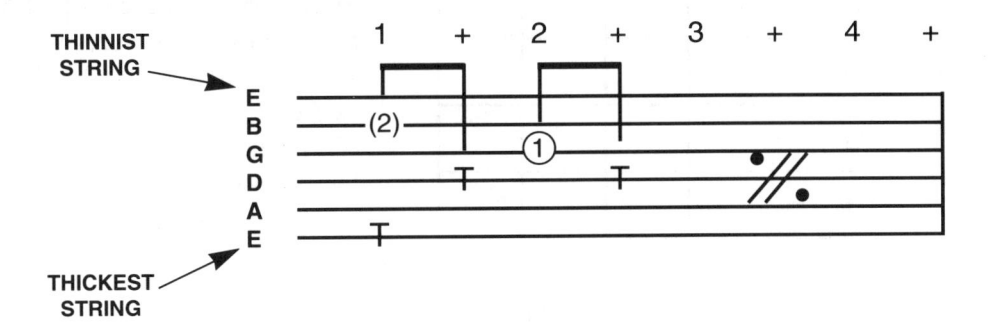

```
THINNIST            1   +   2   +   3   +   4   +
STRING →
          E ─────────────────────────────────────
          B ────(2)──────────────────────────────
          G ──────────────1──────────•───────────
          D ──────T───────T──────────//──────────
          A ─────────────────────────•───────────
          E ────T────────────────────────────────
THICKEST ↗
STRING
```

- Place your fingers on the fretboard for the chord of E.
- Before playing the pattern, find out which fingers will be plucking which strings.
- The first beat is played by the thumb and second finger simultaneously. The thumb plays the thick E string and finger 2 plays the B string. *Note:* The note played by finger 2 is not absolutely essential, hence the brackets.
- The next note is played by the thumb on the D string.
- Next is the main accent of the pattern (denoted by the circle) played by finger 1.
- Lastly, the thumb plays the D string.
- These four notes are then repeated (denoted by the sign ⁄⁄.).

Practise procedure (Cassette example 33)

Now that you've worked out which finger plucks which string, you're ready to play the pattern in time:

- Start counting '1 and 2 and' very slowly.
- Begin playing in time to the count. If you go wrong, it's because you've set too fast a speed for yourself.
- Make sure the accented notes (fingered numbers in circles) are much louder than the rest.
- As you are able to speed up the pattern, the accented notes should maintain the same volume throughout. This applies to the other notes as well, of course.

Important note (Cassette example 34)

In the table, you will notice that for each of the seven fingerpicking patterns, I've not used just one chord to show how each pattern works but three chords (E, A and D). This is because for some chords, the thumb must pluck the E string (6th) as its bass note, whereas other chords must use the A string (5th) and still others the D string (4th).

To find out which string you pluck as the bass note of a given chord, use this chord chart:

```
STRINGS      6    5    4    3    2    1
             E    A    D    G    B    E
    NUT →   ┌────┬────┬────┬────┬────┐
             F    B♭
             ├────┼────┼────┼────┼────┤
   FRETS    F#    B
             ├────┼────┼────┼────┼────┤
             G    C
             ├────┼────┼────┼────┼────┤
             G#   C#
             └────┴────┴────┴────┴────┘
```

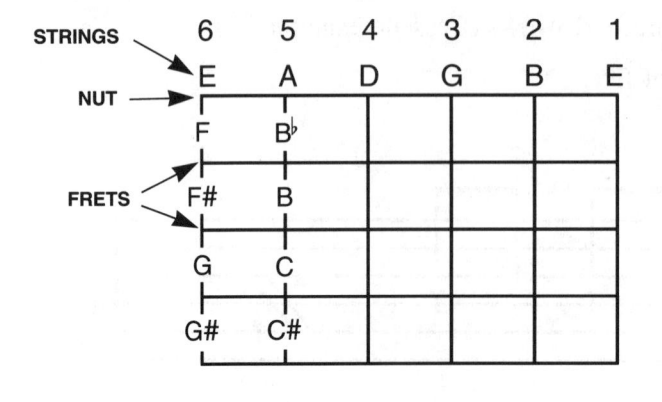

Example: Let's say you want to fingerpick the chord of C and you're not sure which string the thumb should pluck as the bass of C. Find the note 'C' in the chord chart. It's on the A string (5th). Position your fingers for the chord of C thus:

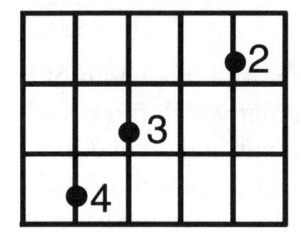

Pluck the A string. This gives you the correct bass note for the chord of C. (Cassette example 35)

Other helpful tips

- Grow the fingernails of your picking hand. Nails on strings sound so much better than skin.
- Keep the nails of your other hand very short.
- If you are fingerpicking in fast songs, keep your playing simple so that you can concentrate your efforts on bringing out the main accents. This is why I've kept patterns 5, 6 and 7 simple.
- To practise the seven fingerpicking patterns, use the seven songs in the section on strumming. Remember to follow the principles of practice found there.
- The best way to improve your fingerpicking and strumming technique is to listen closely to the patterns on the cassette which accompanies this book.

TABLE OF 7 FINGERPICKING PATTERNS
(Cassette example 36)

The reason each pattern has been written out three times is as follows: The chord of E represents all the chords which have their bass note on the E string (6th). When a chord uses the A string or the D string for the bass note of its chord, then the pattern uses slightly different strings.

SPEED	STYLE	TIME SIGNATURE	SONG EXAMPLE	PATTERN NUMBER	PLAY THE CHORD OF E	PLAY THE CHORD OF A	PLAY THE CHORD OF D
Lively	Celebration, Country	4/4	Ah, Lord God	1			
Slow	Worshipful, Ballad	4/4	I just want to praise You	2			
Slow	Worshipful, Ballad	3/4	Abba, Father	3			
Medium	Worship/praise	6/8	An army of ordinary people	4			
Lively	Paise, Rock / Triplet feel	4/4	Thank You, Jesus	5			
Lively	Celebration, Rock	4/4	I am a new creation	6			
Lively	Marches, Hebrew	4/4	I will build My church	7			

6. Bar Chords

Example: B♭maj7

Place your index finger firmly on the fretboard, while at the same time checking to see that the strings aren't buzzing by strumming the strings very slowly.

When you've done that, place the other fingers into position and strum again, checking that no strings are buzzing.

At first this is a very difficult position to hold for any length of time, as the fingers and wrist are likely to ache. This is a natural reaction on the part of muscles that have not been stretched before, so don't worry. But you're going to have to master it some time, so why not start now?

It is worth considering that it will probably take you several months to master the technique of the bar chord.

Basic types of bar chords

Most bar chords are based on one of two groups of chords.

Group 1

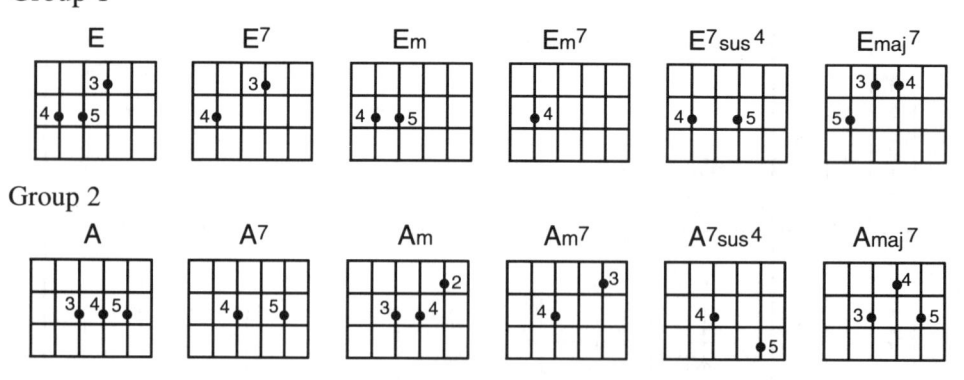

E   E7   Em   Em7   E7sus4   Emaj7

Group 2

A   A7   Am   Am7   A7sus4   Amaj7

It is important to use the correct fingering (index = 1) for this particular section only. It will help you to understand how bar chords are constructed.

Keyboard chart

This chart will help you in working out how bar chords are formulated.
Note that A#, C#, D#, F# and G# are black notes.

```
         A#        C#  D#        F#  G#
    Ⓐ    B    C    D   Ⓔ    F    G    A
    |                  |
    Group 2            Group 1

    <— — — <— — — <— — — <— — — <— — — <—  look to the left
```

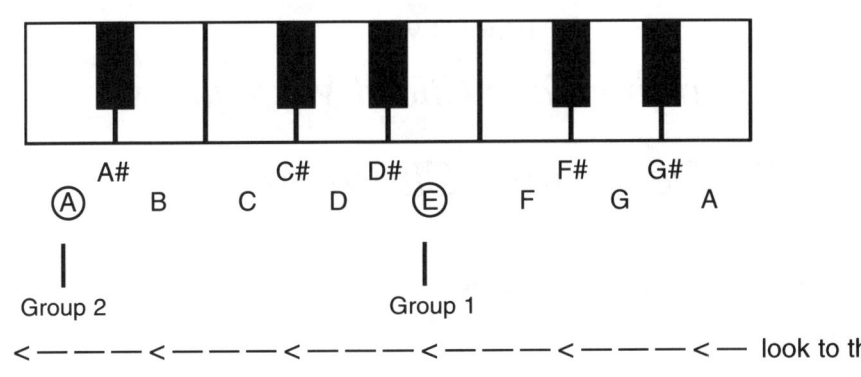

How to use the chart
If you're not sure what the position and fingering are for a particular bar chord simply look to the *left* of the bar chord you're requiring. If you come to Ⓐ first, then you base your bar chord round the A shape. Alternatively, if you come to Ⓔ first, the bar chord would be based round the E shape.

For example, let's say you didn't know what C#m7 was.
1. Look at the note of C# on the keyboard chart.
2. Move your eye to the *left*. You find you come to Ⓐ first. This means that the shape of the C#m7 bar chord will be based on Am7.
3. Place your fingers in the Am7 shape (see Group 2) and move it up the fretboard four places. Why four places? Well, there are four moves from A to C# in the keyboard chart:

    A A# B C C#
    0 1   2 3 4

4. C#m7 is therefore:

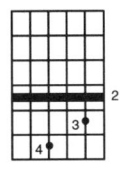

Here is another example. Let's say you didn't know what F#7 was.
1. Look at the note of F# on the keyboard chart.
2. Move to the *left*. You come to Ⓔ first. This means that the shape of the F#7 bar chord is based on E7.
3. Place your fingers in the E7 shape (see Group 1) and move it up the fretboard 2 places. Why 2 places? Because there are 2 moves from E to F# on the keyboard chart, thus:

    E F F#
    0 1 2

4. F#7 is therefore:

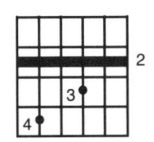

PART TWO

Enlarging Your Chord Vocabulary

7. Decorative Chord Work (1)

Using passing-notes and passing-chords

Passing-notes

Once you have learned some basic chords, the following chord combinations will help you to develop further. For example, if you are playing a section of a song on the chord of A, you can make your playing more interesting by *quickly* moving one or more of your fingers. The effect is of melodic threads being woven in and out of the main chord of A.

For example (Cassette example 37):

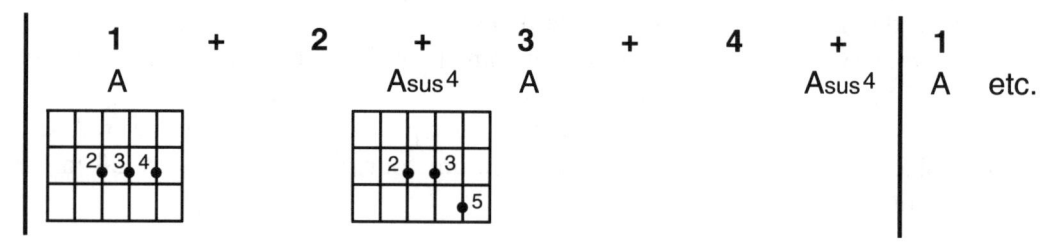

1	+	2	+	3	+	4	+	1
A		Asus4	A			Asus4		A etc.

As long as the moves to Asus4 and away from it are done quickly you could play this move while another guitarist stayed on the chord of A and there wouldn't be a clash of chords.

Passing-chords

Not only can a chord be decorated by moving one or two fingers, but also by moving to another closely related chord, near your basic chord. As with passing-notes, passing chord-moves should be done quickly.

For example: (Cassette example 38)

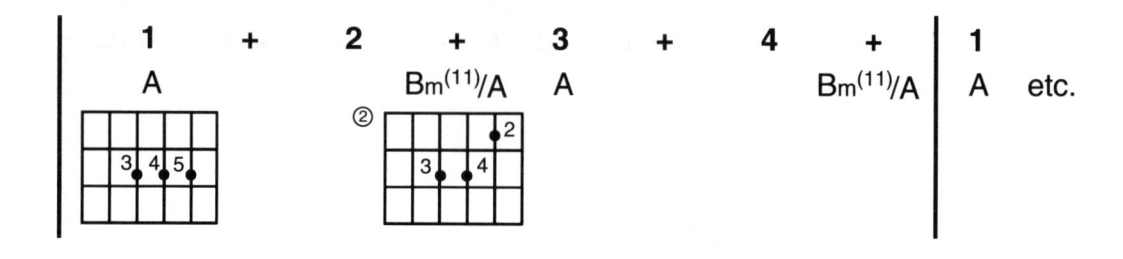

1	+	2	+	3	+	4	+	1
A		Bm$^{(11)}$/A	A			Bm$^{(11)}$/A		A etc.

Note: ② means 'fret 2'. It saves writing out a long chord chart thus:

The fingering for A in the example above is 3, 4 and 5 because it makes it easier to slide to Bm¹¹/A and then back to A.

At first sight, the lists of chord combinations look extremely complicated, but as long as you work through the lists *slowly*, you shouldn't get bogged down.

I've missed out sharps and flats so that you can concentrate on the basic chords. These moves are graded for three levels of ability, beginners, intermediate and advanced.

Other shorthand signs used

- A chord written like this D/F# means this is the chord of D with the bass note of F#. For pianists this direction means that their right hand plays the chord of D and their left hand plays an F# bass note.
- The horizontal line in certain chords represents the *index* finger. For example:

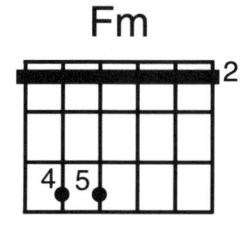

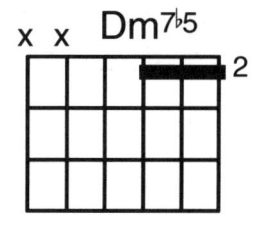

Fm   or   Dm7♭5

- X means 'don't play that string'.

Example No	Standard: Beginner (B) Intermediate (I) Advanced (A)	CHORD COMBINATIONS BASED ROUND A major (Cassette example 39)	Use
1	B	A – Aadd2 – A – Asus4 – A – A6 – A – Aadd11 – A – A9add11 – A	Decorating A
2	A	A – Asus4 – A – Aadd2 – A – A6 – A – A/C# – A	Decorating A
3	I	A – Asus4 – A – A6 – A – Aadd2 – A	Decorating A
4	B	A7* – A7(add13) – A7 – A7(add13) – A7 – A7sus4 – A – A9 – A	Decorating A7
5	I	(chord diagrams leading to D)	Use a few of these chords up to the commas to decorate A7
6	I	(chord diagrams leading to Dm)	Use a few of these chords up to the commas to decorate A7
7	A	A7 – A7sus4 – A7 – A9 – A	Before the chord of D
8	A	A7 – A7sus4 – A7(♭13)	Before the chord of Dm or when in a minor key

42

CHORD COMBINATIONS BASED ROUND A major (continued)

Example No	Standard: Beginner (B) Intermediate (I) Advanced (A)	Chords	Use
9	A	A⁷ – A⁷sus4 – A⁷ A⁷ – A⁷sus4 – A⁷ (Also,)	Decorating A⁷
10	A	Aadd2 – Asus4(add2) – Aadd2 – A(double the 2nd) – Aadd2	Instead of A
11	B	Amaj7 – Amaj7(add13) – Amaj7 – Amaj7(sus4) – Amaj7	Decorating Amaj⁷
12	B	Amaj7 – Dm9/A – Asus9 – Dm9/A – Asus9 – Amaj7	Decorating the last chord in a song
13	I	Amaj7 – Dmaj7/A – Amaj7 Amaj7 – B♭maj7/A – Amaj7 (Also,)	Ending of a song
14	B	A⁶ – G⁶ – D	Ending of a song
15	B	A¹¹ – D Also, A¹¹ – A – D	A¹¹ can be a substitute for A⁷
16	B	A⁷(♭13) – A⁷ – Dm (or D)	Decorating A⁷
17	B	A⁷(♭13) – A⁷(add13) – D	Decorating A⁷

43

Example No	Standard: Beginner (B) Intermediate (I) Advanced (A)	CHORD COMBINATIONS BASED ROUND A major (continued)	Use
18	I	A7(♭13) – A7 – Dm	Decorating A7 in a minor key
19	I	A7(♭13) – A7(♭9) – Dm	Decorating A7 in a minor key
20	I	A7(♭9) – A7(♭9) – A7(♭9) – A7(♭9) – Dm	Decorating a diminished chord
21	B	A – C/A – D/A – A	End of a song
22	I	A – C/A – D/A – A	End of a song
23	B	A – D/A – E/A – A	Singing in the Spirit
24	A	A – D/A – E/A – A	End of a song
25	B	A – B♭/A – B/A – B♭/A – A	End of a song

44

Example No	Standard: Beginner (B) Intermediate (I) Advanced (A)	CHORD COMBINATIONS BASED ROUND A major (continued)	Use
26	A	A – B♭/A – B/A – B♭/A – A	End of a song
27	B	A – B♭/A – C/A – B♭/A – A	End of a song
28	A	A – B♭/A – C/A – B♭/A – A	End of a song
29	I	A – Em7/A – Fmaj7/A – Em7/A – A	End of a song
30	I	A – B/A – D/A – A	End of a song
31	A	A – Bm7sus4/A – Amaj7 – D/A – E/A – A	Singing in the Spirit. ⊖▶ means move quickly away from that chord

45

CHORD COMBINATIONS BASED ROUND A minor
(Cassette example 40)

Example No	Standard: Beginner (B) Intermediate (I) Advanced (A)	Chords	Use
1	B	Am – Am^{add2} – Am – Am^{sus4} – Am	Decorating Am
2	I	Am – Am^{add11} – Am – Am$^{sus\flat6}$ – Am	Decorating Am
3	B	Am – Am^6 – Am^7 – Am^6 – Am	Decorating Am
4	B	Am – Am^{add11} – Am – Am^7 – Am^{add2} – Am^7 – Am	Decorating Am
5	I	Am – Am/C – Am/G – Am	Decorating Am
6	B	Am – E/A – Am	Decorating Am
7	B	Am – A^{9add11}	Decorating Am
8	I	Am – Am$^{\#7}$ – Am^7 – Am$^{\#7}$ – Am	Needs to be played as a progression in its own right

46

Example No	Standard: Beginner (B) Intermediate (I) Advanced (A)	CHORD COMBINATIONS BASED ROUND A minor (continued)	Use
9	A	Am – Am^{add2} – Am – Am$^{\flat13}$ – Am – Am^{sus4} – Am	Decorating Am
10	A	Am – Am^7 – Am	Decorating Am
11	A	Am – Am^7 – Am – Am^{add11} – Am	Decorating Am
12	A	Am – Am$^{\#7}$ – Am	Decorating Am
13	I	Am^7 – D$^{(9)add11}$ – Am^7	Decorating Am^7
14	I	Am^7 – Am^{add2}	To G or to D → D^{sus4}
15	I	Am$^{7\flat5}$	Songs in the key of G: when the song has ended, use the chord of G, go to Am$^{7\flat5}$ then back to G
16	I	Am^{add2} – Am$^{(9)\flat13}$ – Am^{add2}	Dressing up the final chord of Am – best with fingerpicking

47

CHORD COMBINATIONS BASED ROUND B major
(Cassette example 41)

Example No	Standard: Beginner (B) Intermediate (I) Advanced (A)	Chords	Use
1	B	B – B – B	Decorating B
2	A	B – Badd2 – Bsus4 – B	Decorating B
3	A	B – B – B	Decorating B
4	A	B – Aadd2 – E	Use this move in the key of E like this: E–Aadd2–B–E
5	B	B7 – B7/A – B7 – B7/F# – B7	Pick out the bass notes
6	B	B7 – B7sus4 – B7 – B7	Decorating B7
7	A	B7 – B7add2 – B7 – B7sus4 – B7 – B13 – B7 – B7add11	Decorating B7
8	A	B7 – B7sus4 – B7 – B7add11 – B7	Decorating B7
9	A	Bmaj7 – Bmaj9 – Bmaj7 – Bmaj7	Decorating Bmaj7

48

CHORD COMBINATIONS BASED ROUND B minor
(Cassette example 42)

Example No	Standard: Beginner (B) Intermediate (I) Advanced (A)	Chords	Use
1	B	Bm – Bm – Bm – Bm	Decorating Bm
2	A	Bm – F#/B – Bm – Bm	Decorating Bm
3	A	Bm – Bm$^{\#7}$ – Bm^7 – Bm$^{\#7}$ – Bm	Play this as a progression in its own right
4	A	Bm – A^{add2} – Bm	Decorating Bm
5	I	Bm – Bm$^{\#7}$ – Bm	Decorating Bm
6	I	Bm^7 – Bm^7 – Bm^7 – Bm^7 – Bm^7	Decorating Bm^7
7	A	Bm^7 – Bm^7 – Bm^7	Decorating Bm^7

Example No	Standard: Beginner (B) Intermediate (I) Advanced (A)	CHORD COMBINATIONS BASED ROUND C major (Cassette example 43)	Use
1	B	C – C – C – Cadd2 – C – – C – Csus4 – C – – C – G6/C – C	Decorating C
2	B	C – E/C	Ending a song
3	I	C – Dm/C – G7/C – C	A sequence for singing in tongues
4	A	C – Dm/C – Dm7♭5/C – C	Ending a song
5	I	C7 – C7/G Do this move up 2 frets. Then it becomes D7 – D7/A. Then repeat it up another 2 frets which makes the move E – E7/B; up another 2 frets F#7 – F#7/C#, then up another 3 frets (A7 – A7/E). Pick the bass out clearly.	
6	B	Cadd2 – C – Csus4 – C – – C	Decorating C7
7	A	C7 – – C7	Decorating C7

50

CHORD COMBINATIONS BASED ROUND C major (continued)

Example No	Standard: Beginner (B) Intermediate (I) Advanced (A)	Chords	Use
8	A	C^7 — — C^7	Decorating C^7
9	A	C^7 — — C^7 — C^7sus4 — C^7 — C^{13} — C^7	Decorating C^7
10	A	C^7 — C^7sus4 — C^7 — C — C^7 — — C^7	Decorating C^7
11	I	C^9 — Try this move: $Am - C^9 - F^{maj7}$	Use C^9 as a substitute for C^7
12	A	C^9/G — Do this move up 2 frets ($D^9 - D^9/A$). Then up another 2 frets ($E^9 - E^9/G\#$). Up another 2 frets ($F\#^9 - F\#^9/C\#$). Up another 3 frets ($A^9 - A^9/E$).	
13	I	C^9 — C^9add2 — C^9 — C — C^9	Decorating C^{add2}
14	B	C^{add2} — C — C^{maj7} — C	
15	A	C^{add2} — C — Am^7 — Am — Dm^7 — Dm^6 — $G^{(9)}$ — G	Use this as a chord sequence in its own right

51

Example No	Standard: Beginner (B) Intermediate (I) Advanced (A)	CHORD COMBINATIONS BASED ROUND C major (continued)	Use
16		Cmaj7 – C – Cadd2 – C	Decorating Cmaj7
17		Cmaj7 – C – Cadd9 – C	Decorating Cmaj7
18		Cmaj7 – Bm7(11) – E	
19		C11 – F E11 - A,　G11 - C,　A11 - D,　B11 - E,　C11 - F,　D11 - G	Eleventh chords (C11) are really a way of making seventh chords (C7) sound stronger… … try some of these other eleventh chords in other keys
		CHORD COMBINATIONS BASED ROUND C minor (Cassette example 44)	
1	A	Cm – Cmadd2 –, Cm – Cm7 – Cm, – Cm –	Decorating Cm
2	A	Cm – G/C – Cm – C7sus4 – Cm	

52

Example No	Standard: Beginner (B) Intermediate (I) Advanced (A)	CHORD COMBINATIONS BASED ROUND D major (Cassette example 45)	Use
1	B	D – Dsus4 – D – Dadd2 – D	Decorating D
2	B	D – Dadd11 – D – – D	Decorating D
3	B	D – Em7 – D	Decorating D
4	B	D – E♭/D – E/D – E♭/D – D	Ending of songs.
5	B	D – D♭/D – D	Ending of a 'country' song but also 'Jailhouse Rock'
6	B	D – A/D – G/D Also, D – G/D – A/D – D	Ending of songs
7	B	D – E/D – A7/D – D	Ending of songs
8	I	D – Em7/D – Dmaj7 – Em7/D – D	Singing in tongues

Also, D – Em7/D – Dmaj7 – G/D – A/D – D

53

Example No	Standard: Beginner (B) Intermediate (I) Advanced (A)	CHORD COMBINATIONS BASED ROUND D major (continued)	Use
9	I	D – Dmaj7 – D – Dadd2 – D Also, D – C/D – D	Different ways of decorating D
10	I	D – G/D – D – C/D – D	Different ways of decorating D
11	I	D/F# – D – D/F# – Dsus4/F# – D – Dadd2/F# – D/F# – D/F#add11 – – D – D6/F# – D/F#	Different ways of decorating D
12	B	D7 – – – – G or Gm	Decorating D7 before moving to G or Gm
13	B	D7 – D7sus4 – D7 – D9 – D7	Decorating D7
14	B	D7 – – D7 – – D7 – – D7	Decorating D7
15	A	D7 – D7add2 – D7	Decorating D7

Example No	Standard: Beginner (B) Intermediate (I) Advanced (A)	CHORD COMBINATIONS BASED ROUND D major (continued)	Use
16	A	D7 – D7sus4 – D7 – Dadd2 – D7 – Dadd11 – D7	Decorating D7
17	A	D7/F# – D7sus4/F# – D7/F# – D9/F# – D7/F# – D7add11/F# – D7/F# – D6/F# – D7	Decorating D7
18	B	Dmaj7 – Em7 – Dmaj7	Decorating Dmaj7
19	I	Dmaj7 – Em7/D – Dmaj7 Also, Dmaj7/A – Em7/G – Dmaj7/A – D6	Decorating Dmaj7
20	A	Dmaj7 – Dmaj9 – Dmaj7	Decorating Dmaj7

CHORD COMBINATIONS BASED ROUND D minor
(Cassette example 46)

Example No	Standard: Beginner (B) Intermediate (I) Advanced (A)	Chord Progression	Use
1	B	Dm – Dmsus4 – Dm – Dmadd2 – Dm – Dmadd11 – Dm – Dmsus4(add2) – Dm	Decorating Dm
2	B	Dm – A/D – Gadd2/D – A7/D – Dm	Song ending
3	I	Dm – Dm/F – Dmadd2/F – A7sus4 – A7 – Dm	Singing in tongues
4	A	Dm – Dm#7 – Dm7 – Dm#7 – Dm	Decorating Dm
5	A	Dm – Em/D – Dm7 – G/D – Dm7 – Em/D – Dm	Singing in tongues
6	A	Dm – Dmaug – Dm6 – Dmaug – Dm	End of a song
7	B	Dm – Dm7♭5 – C	Ending a song in the key of C
8	B	Dm – Dmadd2 – Dm. Also, Dm – Em/D – Dm	Ending a song in the key of Dm

56

Example No	Standard: Beginner (B) Intermediate (I) Advanced (A)	CHORD COMBINATIONS BASED ROUND D minor (continued)	Use
9	B	Dm⁹	Used as a final chord instead of Dm
10	A	Dm – Dm^add2 – Dm – A/D – Dm – Dm^add11 – Dm – Gm⁶/D	Decorating Dm

		CHORD COMBINATIONS BASED ROUND E major (Cassette example 47)	
1	B	E – E^add2 – E – E⁶ – E – E^sus4 – E	Decorating E
2	B	E – E⁷ – E – E^add11 – E	Decorating E
3	I	E – F#m⁷/E – E^maj7 – E – F#m⁷/E	Singing in tongues
4	B	E – B^add11/E – A^add2/E – E	Singing in tongues
5	I	E – F#m⁷♭5/E	Ending a song
6	I	E – A^add2/E – B^add11/E – E	Playing the E with different fingering enables you to slide to interesting versions of A and B
7	I	E – Bm⁷add11/E – E	Decorating E

57

CHORD COMBINATIONS BASED ROUND E major (continued)

Example No	Standard: Beginner (B) Intermediate (I) Advanced (A)	Chords	Use
8	B	E7 – E7sus4 – E7 – E7add13 – E7 – E9 – E7 – E7sus4(add13) – E7 E7sus4(add2) – E7 – E7add11 – E7	Decorating E
9	I	E7 – – – – – – A	Use some or all of these chords to decorate E7 before moving on
10	I	E7 – – – – – Am	Use these to decorate E7 before moving to Am
11	I	Emaj7 – F#m7/E – E Also, Emaj7 – E7 – F#m7/E – F#m♭5/E – E	Ending a song
12	A	Emaj7* – Emaj7 – Emaj7* – F#m7/E* – F#m7/E – F#m7/E*	
13	I	E – Aadd2*/E – Aadd2/E – Aadd2*/E – A6/E – Aadd2*/E – Badd11/E – E	A big ending to a song
14	A	E11 – A. Also, E11 – A. Also, E11 – A	Sometimes E7 can sound a bit bare, so E11 is an alternative as you close a song in A

58

CHORD COMBINATIONS BASED ROUND E minor
(Cassette example 48)

Example No	Standard: Beginner (B) Intermediate (I) Advanced (A)	Chords	Use
1	I	Em – Em^{add3} – Em^{add2} – Em – Em^7 – Em$^{\#6}$ – Em – Em^{sus4} – Em	Decorate Em
2	B	Em – Em^{add11} – Em – Em^7 – Em – Em^{7add11} – Em	Decorate Em
3	I	Em – Em^{add6} – Em – Em^{sus4} – Em – Em$^{sus4(add6)}$ – Em	Decorate Em
4	I	Em – Em/F# – Em/G – Em/F# – Em	Emphasise the bass notes
5	B	Em – Em^{add6} – Em^{add2} – Em	Decorating Em
6	B	Em – Em – Em^{7sus4} – Em^{add6} – Em^{add2}	Decorating Em
7	I	Em – Em$^{\#7}$ – Em^7 – Em$^{\#7}$ – Em	Decorating Em
8	I	Em – Bm^{sus4}/E – C^{maj7}/E – Bm^{sus4}/E – Em	Decorating Em
9	I	Em – Em$^{\#6add2}$ – Em^7 – Em$^{\#6add2}$ – Em	Decorating Em

Example No	Standard: Beginner (B) Intermediate (I) Advanced (A)	CHORD COMBINATIONS BASED ROUND E minor (continued)	Use
10	I	Em^{add2} – C^{maj7}/E – Bm^{sus4}/E – Em	Singing in tongues (warfare context)
11		Em^{add2} – Em^{6add2} – Em$^{\#6add2}$ – Em^{6add2} – Em^{add2}	Decorating the last chord of a song in Em

		CHORD COMBINATIONS BASED ROUND F major (Cassette example 49)	
1	B	F – F^{add2} – F – F^{sus4} – F – F^{add6} – F – F$^{(add\flat5)}$ – F	Decorating F
2	I	F – F^{add2} – F – F^{sus4} – F – F^{add6} – F – F$^{(add2)}$ – F	Decorating F
3	A	F – F^{add11} – F	Decorating F
4	B	F^{maj7} – F^{maj9} – F^{maj7} – F$^{maj7add\#11}$ – F^{maj7} – F$^{maj9add\#11}$ – F^{maj7}	Decorating F^{maj7}
5	I	(This is a helpful version of Fmaj7 to master, if you find the F bar chord too hard) F^{maj7} – F^{maj9} – F^{maj7} – F$^{maj7add\#11}$ – F^{maj7} – F$^{maj9add\#11}$ – F^{maj7} (quick move)	Decorating F^{maj7}
6	A	F^{7}/E$^\flat$ – F^{7sus4}/E$^\flat$ – F^{7}/E$^\flat$ – F^{6}/E$^\flat$ – F^{7}/E$^\flat$ – F^{9}/E$^\flat$ – F^{7}/E$^\flat$	Decorating F^{7}

Example No	Standard: Beginner (B) Intermediate (I) Advanced (A)	CHORD COMBINATIONS BASED ROUND F major (continued)	Use
7		F7 – F9 – F7 – F7add11 – F7 – F7sus4 – F7	Decorating F7
8		Fadd9 – – Fadd9	Decorating F7

CHORD COMBINATIONS BASED ROUND F minor
(Cassette example 50)

Example No	Level	Chords	Use
1	I	Fm – Fm – Fm – Fm	Decorating Fm
2	A	Fm – Fmsus4 – Fm – Fmaug – Fm – Fm6 – Fm – B♭m/F – Fm	Decorating Fm
3	A	Fm – Fm6 – Fm – Fm7 – Fm6 – Fm – Fmsus4 – Fm	Decorating Fm
4	A	Fm – Fmadd♭13 – Fm – Fmadd11 – Fm	Decorating Fm
5		Fm – Fm#7 – Fm – Fmadd♭13 – Fm	Decorating Fm
6		Fm6 – Fm – C	Ending a song in C

61

Example No	Standard: Beginner (B) Intermediate (I) Advanced (A)	CHORD COMBINATIONS BASED ROUND G major (Cassette example 51)	Use
1	I	G – G^{sus4} – G – G^{add2} – G – C/G – G – G^{sus4add9} – G (different fingering)	Decorating G
2	I	G – G^{add9} – G – G^6 – G	Decorating G
3	B	G – G^6 – G	Decorating G
4	I	G – G^{aug} – G^6 – G^{aug} – G	Decorating the last chord of a song
5	I	G – C/G – D/G – C/G – G	Singing in tongues
6	A	G – C/G – G^{maj7} – C/G – G	Singing in tongues
7	A	G – C/G – G^{maj9} – C/G – G	Singing in tongues
8	A	G – A^7/G – C/G – G	Decorating the last chord of a song
9	A	G – F/G – C	F/G can be used instead of G^7

Example No	Standard: Beginner (B) Intermediate (I) Advanced (A)	CHORD COMBINATIONS BASED ROUND G major (continued)	Use
10	I	G – G/F – C/E	G/F can be used instead of G^7
11	I	G – C^{add2} – F$^{6(add9)}$ – C^{add2} – G	Wherever you see G and C together, you can replace them with these chords. I've added the F$^{6(add9)}$ to show that the pattern can continue
12	A	G – G^{add11} – G – G^7 – G	Decorating G
13	I	G^7 – G^6 – C. Also, G^7 – G^{13} – C	Instead of moving from G^7 to C, G^6 and G^{13} enrich the move
14	A	G^7 – G^9 – G^7 – G^{13} – G^7 – G^{7sus4} – G^7 G – G^7 – G^{7add11} – G^7	Decorating G^7
15	I	G^{maj7} – G – G^6 – G^{maj7} – G$^{maj7(add8)}$ – G^{maj7}	Decorating G^{maj7}
		CHORD COMBINATIONS BASED ROUND G minor (Cassette example 52)	
1	I	Gm – Gm^{add2} – Gm – – –Gm– Gm^{sus4} – Gm	Decorating Gm

63

CHORD COMBINATIONS BASED ROUND G minor
(continued)

Example No	Standard: Beginner (B) Intermediate (I) Advanced (A)	Chords	Use
2	A	Gm – Gm⁹ – Gm – Gm⁷ – Gm⁷⁽ᵃᵈᵈ⁶⁾ – Gm⁷⁽ᵃᵈᵈ♭⁶⁾ – Gm	Decorating Gm
3	A	Gm – Gm⁷ – Gm – Gmᵃᵈᵈ¹¹ – Gm – Gm⁷⁽ᵃᵈᵈ¹¹⁾ – Gm (play quickly)	Play the chords before Gm quickly and back on to Gm
4	B	Gm⁶/D – D	A decorated ending in the key of D
5		GmD – D	A decorated ending in the key of D

8. Decorative Chord Work (2)

Using bass note passing-chords

These chords will be marked with an asterisk, eg

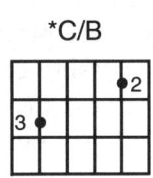

When you are moving from one chord to another, by simply moving one or two fingers, you can form a new chord half-way between. We will call this a 'passing-chord'. This has the same effect as the chords in Chapter 7 had, of weaving melodies in between chords, only this time you are required to pick out the bass note of the chord. To help you pick out the correct bass note in a chord, the string you must emphasise as you strum will be marked with an arrow, thus:

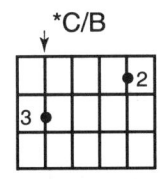

How this method works (Cassette example 53)

Let's say you are playing the song *Jesus, we enthrone You* and the opening chords are G to Em. Below we show how to make this move sound more interesting by putting in the passing-chord – G/F#.

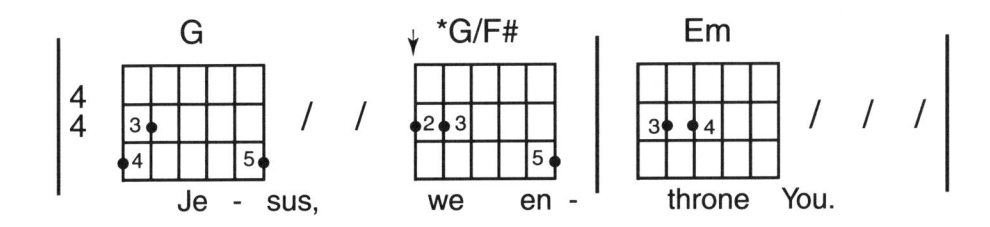

Because these 'passing-chords' are only acting like stepping stones between two points, you must not remain on them for more than one or two beats, especially if you are playing with other musicians who, in the above example, may simply be playing | G /// | Em /// |, otherwise a dissonance will result.

How to use the bass note passing-chord tables

Chords are dealt with in alphabetical order, A to G (major and minor). For example, as you look at the first group of chords based round the letter A, you will see that chords are grouped 1(a), (b), (c); 2(a), (b), etc. This is done so that chords with a similar bass note are in the same group; ie, 1(a) A–G#–F#, 2(a) A–G–F# etc.

To explain this, look at 1(a). Here the progression is A to F#m with a passing-chord of *A/G#. 2(a) is also the move A to F#m but this time, the passing-chord's bass note is G, not G#. If you are playing a song and you see the move A to F#m and want to decorate it with a passing-chord, you might well wonder which one you should use. The simple answer is, the one which sounds correct – because one will sound incorrect. So quickly try out both ways. Whenever you're not sure, look at the Table of Keys in which that passing-chord is best used. For instance, as you compare 1(a) and 2(a), you will notice that the passing-chord *A/G# shouldn't be used in the key of E minor. *A/G is more appropriate in that key.

To help you further, at the back of the *Songs of Fellowship* book, there is a song index with the key of each song next to the song title, though this is for pianists. For example, most guitarists would not play in A♭, they would play in G with capo 1.

Bracketed chords

Some progressions are extended with chords in brackets, eg, 3(b) Am–*Am/G–Am/F#–(Fmaj7–E–Am). This is done so that you can see how the passing-chords fit into a broad passage of music.

Some easy examples of how to use the passing-chords in songs

(*Note*: Numbers such as 8(a) over the passing-chords refer to their place in the chord progression tables a few pages further on.)

1. *Do not strive* (SoF 325) Starting at bar 7 (Cassette example 54):

```
                              8(a)         3(a)
     | F  /  G  /   | C   *C/B   Am   *Am/G  | Dm
...For| mine is the power and the | glo  -    ry        for- | ever ...
```

2. *When I feel the touch* (SoF 594) Starting at bar 1 (Cassette example 55):

14(a)	6(a)	17(d)	2(b)
D / *D/C /	B⁷ / *B⁷/A /	Em / *Em/D /	A / *A/G /
When I feel the	touch of your	hand u - pon my	life it causes

14(b)	14(b)		
D / *D/C /	G/B /*Gm/B♭/	D/A / A⁷ /	D
me to sing a	song that I	love you	Lord.

Note: In bar 6, I have changed the chord of G to G/B. Occasionally, you may have to change the chords slightly to incorporate the passing-chord's bass notes, eg, change C to C/E, C to C/G, D to D/A, D to D/F#, G to G/B, G7 to G7/B etc.

3. *I will seek Your face* (SoF 276) Starting at bar 3 (Cassette example 56):

	7(a)	19(a)	17(d)
Bm / / /	/ /*Bm/A /	G / / *G/F#	Em / /*Em/D
... O Lord.		I will	seek your face, O

	2(b)		
A / / /	/ / *A/G /	*D/F#	
Lord.		I ...	

4. *River, wash over me* (SoF 487) Starting at bar 6 (Cassette example 57):

	8(a)	15(b)		
G⁷ / / C	/ *C/B	A⁷ / A⁷/G	Dm / Dm/C	G⁷/B / G⁷	C
make me new.		Bathe me re-	fresh me	and fill me ...

Note: Whenever the move Dm (or Dm7) to G (or G7) occurs, you can use 15(b), eg, bar 3 on *Do not strive* (SoF 325).

5. *Seek ye first* (SoF 493) Starting at bar 3 (Cassette example 58):

	20(a)	
F / C /	G / G/F /	C/E
... and His righteous-	ness.	and ...

Example number	Standard (Adv/Inter/Beg)	CHORD PROGRESSION (Cassette example 59)	The guitar key of a song where this example can usually be used												
			A	Am	B	Bm	C	D	Dm	E	Em	F	F#m	G	Gm
1(a)	A	A – *A/G# – F#m	•		•	•		•		•			•		
(b)	A	A – *A/G# – F#m – [F#m/E – D]	•		•	•				•			•		
(c)	A	A – *A/G# – D/F#	•		•	•				•			•		
2(a)	A	A(or A^7) – *A/G(or A^7/G) – F#m	•		•		•			•			•		
(b)	I	A(or A^7) – *A/G(or A^7/G) – D/F# (or D or Dm)	•		•		•						•		
3(a)	I	Am – Am/G(or Am^7/G) – D/F# (or D)	•		•	•	•			•	•		•		
(b)	I	Am – *Am/G – Am/F# – [F^{maj7} – E – Am]	•			•	•		•				•		
(c)	I	Am – *Am/G – [F^{maj7} – (or F, or Dm)]	•			•		•			•				
4	I	Am – *Em/G – F^{maj7} (or F)		•		•		•		•			•		

Example number	Standard(Adv/Inter/Beg)	CHORD PROGRESSION	A	Am	B	Bm	C	D	Dm	E	Em	F	F#m	G	Gm
5(a)	A	B – *B/A – G#m	•		•					•			•		
(b)	A	B – *B/A – G	•	•		•									
(c)	A	B – *B/A – E (or Em)	•	•	•	•					•		•		
6(a)	I	B7 – *B7/A – G#m	•		•					•					
(b)	B	B7 – *B7/A – G	•	•		•	•				•			•	
(c)	B	B7 – *B7/A – E (or Em)	•	•	•	•					•		•		
7(a)	I	Bm – *Bm/A – G	•			•	•			•	•				
(b)	I	Bm – *Bm/A – E (or Em)	•			•				•	•		•		
8(a)	B	C – *C/B – Am (or Am7)		•		•	•	•			•	•		•	•
(b)	B	C – *C/B – A (or A7)						•	•					•	
9(a)	I	C – *A7/B♭ – A7					•	•			•			•	
(b)	A	C – *A7/B♭ – Dm7/A – [*Dm7♭5/A♭ – C/G – G7/C					•	•	•		•			•	
10(a)	I	C – *G/B – Am7		•			•	•	•		•			•	
(b)	I	C – *G/B – A (or A7)						•	•		•			•	
(c)	I	C – *G/B – *A7/B♭ – A7						•	•	•					

69

Example number	Standard(Adv/Inter/Beg)	CHORD PROGRESSION	\multicolumn{14}{c}{The guitar key of a song where this example can usually be used}
			A	Am	B	Bm	C	D	Dm	E	Em	F	F#m	G	Gm
11(a)	B	C – *E7/B – Am		•		•	•				•	•			
(b)	B	C – *E7/B – A (or A7)	•				•	•							
12	A	Cm – *Cm/A – G (or Gm)										•		•	•
13(a)	I	D – *D/C# – Bm – [*Bm/A – G – A – D]	•			•		•			•		•		
(b)	I	D – *D/C# – Gmaj7/B – [*D/A – G – A – D]	•			•		•			•		•		
14(a)	I	D – *D/C – B (or B7, Bm, Bm7)		•							•		•		
(b)	I	D – *D/C – G/B – [*Gm/B♭ – D/A – A7 – D]						•					•		
(c)	I	D – *D/C – G/B – (D/A – G)						•					•		
(d)	I	D – *D/C – Gmaj7/B – [*Gm#7/B♭ – D/A – A7 – D]						•					•		
15(a)	I	Dm – *Dm/C – G7/B – [*Gm6/B♭ – A7sus4 – A7 – Dm]							•						•

Example number	Standard(Adv/Inter/Beg)	CHORD PROGRESSION	\multicolumn{14}{c	}{The guitar key of a song where this example can usually be used}

Ex	Std	Chord Progression	A	Am	B	Bm	C	D	Dm	E	Em	F	F#m	G	Gm
(b)	B	Dm – *Dm/C – G7/B – [G7]					•		•						
(c)	I	Dm – *Dm/C – Dm/B – [B♭maj7(11) – A7]							•		•				
(d)	I	Dm – *Dm/C – B♭maj7(11) – [A7]							•		•		•		
16(a)	I	E – *E/D# – C#m		•						•		•			
(b)	I	E – *E/D# – C#m		•						•		•			
(c)	I	E – *E/D – C#m	•			•	•			•					
17(a)	I	Em – *Em/D# – *Em/D – *Em/C# – Cmaj7	•				•				•			•	
(b)	I	Em – *Em/D – *Em/C# – (Cmaj7 or C)	•						•					•	•
(c)	I	Em – *Em/D – *Em/C# – (Cmaj7 or C)	•						•			•		•	•
(d)	B	E – *Em/D – C (or A, A7, Am, Am7)					•	•	•		•				

Example number	Standard(Adv/Inter/Beg)	CHORD PROGRESSION	A	Am	B	Bm	C	D	Dm	E	Em	F	F#m	G	Gm
18(a)	B	F (or F^{maj7}) – *F/E – Dm		•			•		•			•		•	•
(b)	I	F (or F^{maj7}) – *F/E – Dm		•			•					•		•	•
19(a)	B	G – *G/F# – Em – [Em^7 – C]	•	•		•		•			•		•	•	
(b)	B	G – *G/F# – C/E	•	•				•			•		•		
(c)	I	G – *G/F# – G/F – (C/E or E or E^7)	•	•			•								
20(a)	I	G – *G/F – C/E		•			•	•	•			•		•	
(b)	I	G – *G/F – E (or E^7)		•			•	•	•						
21(a)	I	Gm – *Gm/E – D (or Dm)						•	•						•
(b)	I	Gm – *Gm/E – A^7 – [Dm or D]	•					•	•						•

72

9. Chord Sequences

Chord sequences can be used in the following ways.

1. To help musicians limber up at the beginning of a rehearsal.
A chord sequence can act as a framework for everyone to improvise in. This can be quite enjoyable! Unfortunately, too many church groups get bogged down with merely rehearsing the 'nuts and bolts' of the songs and they rarely enjoy worshipping and playing together.

2. As a musical interlude in a meeting.
At an appropriate point in the worship (known in Scripture as a 'selah'), the leader may direct the musicians to minister to the people or to the Lord. A sequence helps by providing a repetitive structure to work in.

3. To undergird the worship.
The aim of leading worship is not to get through your list of songs. After a certain song, it may feel right not to rush on but to allow the Holy Spirit to move among the people and for them to bathe in God's presence. A sequence can help to create the space necessary for this to happen.

4. At the ends of songs.
The leader may encourage people to sing out their praises spontaneously to God, or to name the names of God, eg, 'You are my Redeemer, my Saviour,' etc, or the attributes of God, eg, 'You are so strong yet so sensitive,' etc.

5. To accompany singing in tongues.
See the following chapter for further details.

A chord sequence must relate to and build on the mood of the worship.

Here are some sequences in A major and A minor. If you like the sound of a particular sequence but you would rather it was in a different key, then look at the Roman numerals of that sequence and then look at the table of Roman numerals to locate the chords of the sequence in the new key; for example:

	A	–	F#m	–	D	–	E	–
sequence:	A	–	F#m	–	D	–	E	–
Roman numerals:	I	–	VIm	–	IV	–	V	–

Now, look at the table of Roman numerals to find I–VIm–IV–V in other keys.

| The above sequence in the key of G: | G(I) | –Em(VIm) | – | C(IV)– | D(V)– |
| The above sequence in the key of C: | C(I) | –Am(VIm) | – | F(IV)– | G(V)– |

If having transposed a sequence into another key you are now not sure of a chord or two, you should find them under 'chord tables' and 'chord combinations' in previous chapters.

TABLE OF ROMAN NUMERALS

KEY ↓

Scale of key →

I	II	III	IV	V	VI	VII
C	D	E	F	G	A	B
D♭	E♭	F	G♭	A♭	B♭	C
D	E	F#	G	A	B	C#
E♭	F	G	A♭	B♭	C	D
E	F#	G#	A	B	C#	D#
F	G	A	B♭	C	D	E
G♭	A♭	B♭	B	D♭	E♭	F
G	A	B	C	D	E	F#
A♭	B♭	C	D♭	E♭	F	G
A	B	C#	D	E	F#	G#
B♭	C	D	E♭	F	G	A

	CHORD SEQUENCE								ROMAN NUMERAL EQUIVALENTS								Other keys this sequence works well in
	1	2	3	4	1	2	3	4	1	2	3	4	1	2	3	4	
1.	A	/	F#m	/	D	/	E	/	I	/	VIm	/	IV	/	V	/	
2.	A	/	Bm$^{7(11)}$/A	/	A^{maj7}	/	Bm$^{7(11)}$/A	/	I	/	IIm$^{7(11)}$/I	/	Imaj7	/	IIm$^{7(11)}$/I	/	D, E
3.	A	/	E/A	/	D/A	/	E/A	/	I	/	V/I	/	IV/I	/	V/I	/	D, E
4.	A	/	Em^7	/	•//•				I	V^{m7}	/		•//•				D
5.	A	/	G^{maj7}	/	•//•				I	/	♭VII^{maj7}	/	•//•				D
6.	A	/	Em^7	/	G^{maj7}	/	A	/	I	/	V^{m7}	/	♭VII^{maj7}	/	I	/	D
7.	A	/	/	/	F^{maj7}	/	Em^{7sus4}	/	I	/	/	/	♭VI^{maj7}	/	V^{m7sus4}	/	E
8.	A^{maj7}	/	D^{maj7}	/	•//•				I^{maj7}	/	IV^{maj7}	/	•//•				D
9.	A^{sus9}	A	F#m^{sus9}	F#m	Bm^7	Bm^6	E^{sus9}	E	I^{sus9}	I	VIm^{sus9}	VIm	IIm^7	IIm^6	V^{sus9}	V	C
10.	Am	/	G	/	F	/	E	/	Im	/	♭VII	/	VI	/	V	/	
11.	Am	/	C	/	Dm	/	E	/	Im	/	III	/	IVm	/	V	/	Em
12.	Am	/	C	/	D	/	F	/	Im	/	III	/	IV	/	VI	/	Em
13.	Am	/	Em^7	/	•//•				Im	/	V^{m7}	/	•//•				Dm
14.	Am	/	Em^7	/	F^{maj7}	/	G	/	Im	/	V^{m7}	/	VI^{maj7}	/	♭VII	/	
15.	Am^{sus9}	/	Bm$^{7(11)}$/F#	/	C^{maj7}/G	/	Bm$^{7(11)}$/F#	/	Im^{sus9}	/	IIm$^{7(11)}$/#VI	/	III^{maj7}/♭VII	/	IIm$^{7(11)}$/#VI	/	
16.	*Am	/	F/A	/	G/A	/	F/A	/	Im	/	VI/I	/	♭VII/I	/	VI/I	/	Em
17.	Am	/	Bm$^{7(11)}$/A	/	C/A	/	Bm$^{7(11)}$/A	/	Im	/	IIm$^{7(11)}$/I	/	III/I	/	IIm$^{7(11)}$/I	/	Dm
18.	Am^{sus9}	/	/	/	Am$^{sus9(13)}$	/	/	/	Im^{sus9}	/	/	/	Im$^{sus9(13)}$	/	/	/	Em
19.	Am	/	Am$^{#7}$/E	/	Am^7	/	Am$^{#7}$/E	/	Im	/	Im$^{#7}$/V	/	Im^7	/	Im$^{#7}$/V	/	Dm

Chords used in the above sequences (Cassette example 60)

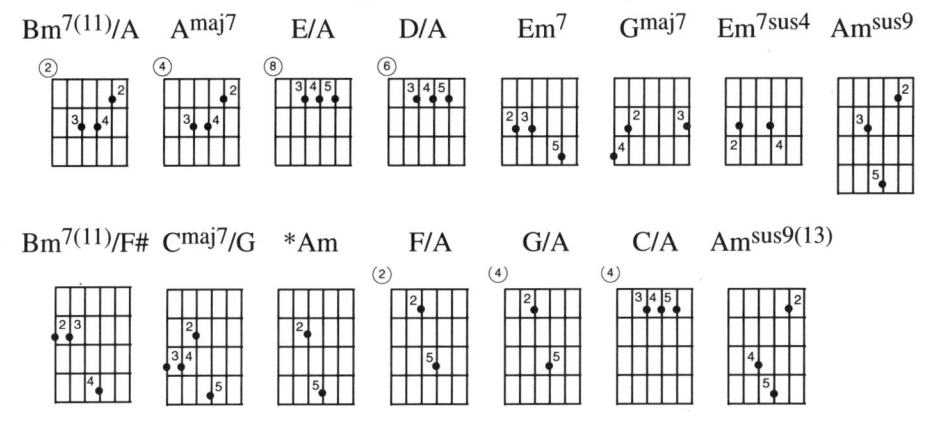

Bm$^{7(11)}$/A   A^{maj7} E/A   D/A   Em^7 G^{maj7} Em^{7sus4} Am^{sus9}

Bm$^{7(11)}$/F#   C^{maj7}/G   *Am   F/A   G/A   C/A   Am$^{sus9(13)}$

10. *Singing in Tongues*

Guidelines for a leader

1. Encourage the people to see that all singing, whether in our native tongue or not, should be governed by our *will*, not by our *feelings*. There is nothing in the Greek original which suggests that speaking or singing in tongues has anything to do with emotion. It is a mistake to think that warm 'furry' feelings can help you begin to sing in this way. It is also a misconception to believe that one should become excited or aroused when singing in tongues. The Holy Spirit can be hindered by frenzied emotions just as much as by an obstinate will or an over-cautious intellect. As with all expressions of praise and worship, singing in tongues operates not from our feelings but from our wills. Therefore encourage people not to wait for the right atmosphere to be generated, or to feel prompted by the Holy Spirit before they sing.
2. Get the balance between taking the initiative in starting the singing yourself, and allowing it to emerge from the congregation. In some churches, singing in tongues is unlikely to occur unless the leader gives the people a nudge.
3. Break any habit patterns that may have developed. Don't let things become predictable. Risk experimentation. If there is no development (ie, the same few people sing at the same volume for the same length of time every time), don't be afraid to instruct the congregation as to the various possibilities open to them. Perhaps workshops can be arranged when the fellowship can look afresh at how worship can become more creative in its expression.

The following section looks at some possible ways of enriching our times of singing in tongues.

1. Singing in tongues – using the song melody

The words of the song don't have to be replaced syllable for syllable with the words of your praise language.

The tune of the song should be regarded as a guideline around which you improvise with as few or as many notes as you want.

The mechanics

After singing a song a number of times through, you may feel it is right to lead the people to sing it again. This time, instead of people using the words of the song to accompany the melody, you direct them to sing in tongues. (It may be that no such direction is necessary because as you begin to sing this verse in tongues, people follow your lead.) Should you feel it *would* help the congregation to give a direction, *make it very clear.* Something simple like, 'Singing the tune – with the spirit,' would suffice.

As the singing commences, your vocal lead must be clear but not overpowering. (There is no premium in volume.)

On occasions, I have sensed that people are just beginning to step out and sing in this way when the worship leader suddenly draws things to a close. Any exercise of faith will involve a momentary 'tug-of-war' between belief and doubt. Singing the tune twice through provides a lengthy enough framework which will enable people to step out and enjoy singing in this way.

After singing the tune in tongues, you could direct people to return to singing the tune for the last time through, this time in their native tongue. If that is so, then simply make an announcement such as, 'In my life, last time.'

Alternatively, having sung the melody in tongues once or twice, you might draw the song to a close at that point.

A further option, after the tune has been sung in tongues, is to allow it to carry on without any main melody or accompaniment from the musicians.

Note: In each of the alternatives above, the worship leader must always be prepared to take a reliable lead.

2. Singing in tongues – at the end of a song

As the last chord of a song dies away, singing in tongues may occur. It may emerge from the body of the congregation or be started by the worship leader. If the musicians are to accompany the singing, they might consider the following.

(a) Play one chord without a definite rhythm.

As the singing in tongues begins, the musicians may wait for a few bars before playing quietly on the tonic chord (eg, if the song is in the key of G major, the tonic chord is G).

For example: *Living under the shadow of His wing* (SoF 346) (Cassette example 61)

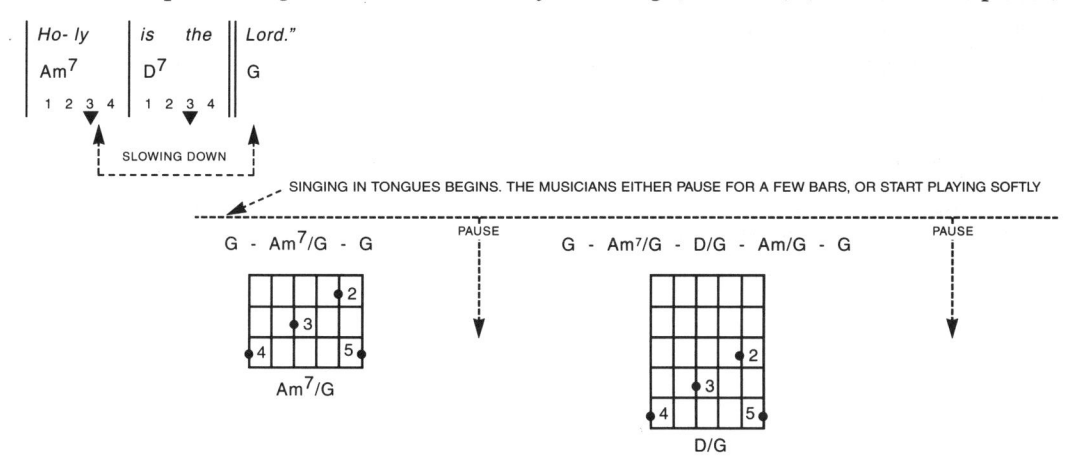

Ho- ly	is the	Lord."
Am⁷	D⁷	G
1 2 3 4	1 2 3 4	

SLOWING DOWN

SINGING IN TONGUES BEGINS. THE MUSICIANS EITHER PAUSE FOR A FEW BARS, OR START PLAYING SOFTLY

G - Am⁷/G - G   PAUSE   G - Am⁷/G - D/G - Am/G - G   PAUSE

Am⁷/G

D/G

GUITAR PLAYS THE CHORDS ABOVE, WHILE ANOTHER GUITAR AND PIANO PLAY THE CHORD OF G
(NO REGULAR RHYTHM, SO NO BAR LINES NEEDED)

The root key of this singing is likely to be G, since the key of the song that has been sung is G.

As the singing in tongues continues, one guitar and piano can play the chord of G softly, while the other guitar plays the suggested chords. These moving chords of G–Am7/G–G will not clash with the basic root chord of G being played on the piano and other guitar *if the chords are played quickly, like passing-chords, always returning to G.*

To see how you would do these moves in other keys, refer back to 'chord tables' and 'chord combinations'.

Alternatively, as the musicians continue to improvise in G, the guitarist can use the following chords as alternatives to those in the above example.

Note: Emphasise the top/thinner strings.

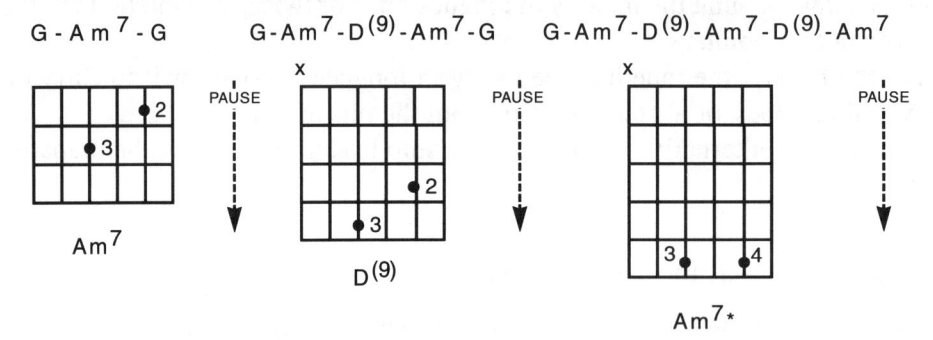

G - Am^7 - G   G - Am^7 - D$^{(9)}$ - Am^7 - G   G - Am^7 - D$^{(9)}$ - Am^7 - D$^{(9)}$ - Am^7

Am^7 D$^{(9)}$ Am^7*

Or any combination of the chords in the previous example can be played like this (Cassette example 62):

Am7–G–Am7–G *pause* D(9)–Am7–D(9)–Am7–G–Am7–G
pause Am7*–D(9)–Am7*–D(9)–Am7–D(9)–Am7–G–Am7–G *pause*

The best way of viewing this decorative chord work is to think of the guitarist's instrument as being equivalent to the vocalist's voice. Just as someone singing in tongues will shape a melody which rises and falls in its contour, so a guitarist is attempting to create similar peaks and troughs with these chords, moving back and forth to G.

(b) Play one chord with a definite rhythm (Cassette example 63)

In this method, as singing in tongues emerges, the musicians accompany with a rhythmic pattern (maybe the same as that of the song). This rhythm may begin softly, becoming more prominent by the use of regular accents.

Here is the last example above, this time played rhythmically:

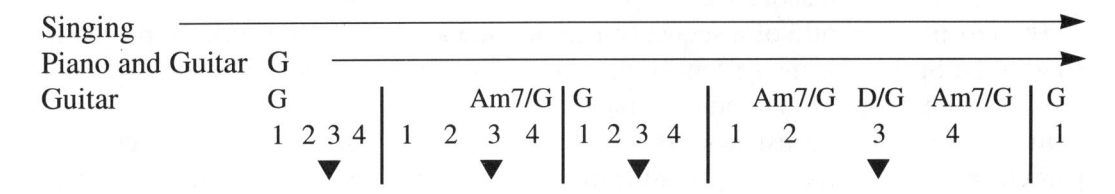

```
Singing            ───────────────────────────────────────────►
Piano and Guitar  G ───────────────────────────────────────────►
Guitar            G         | Am7/G  G    | Am7/G  D/G  Am7/G | G
                  1 2 3 4   | 1  2  3  4  | 1  2  3  4        | 1
                    ▼           ▼      ▼      ▼
```

To demonstrate this in another key, here is the end of the song *Ascribe greatness* (SoF 26) (Cassette example 64).

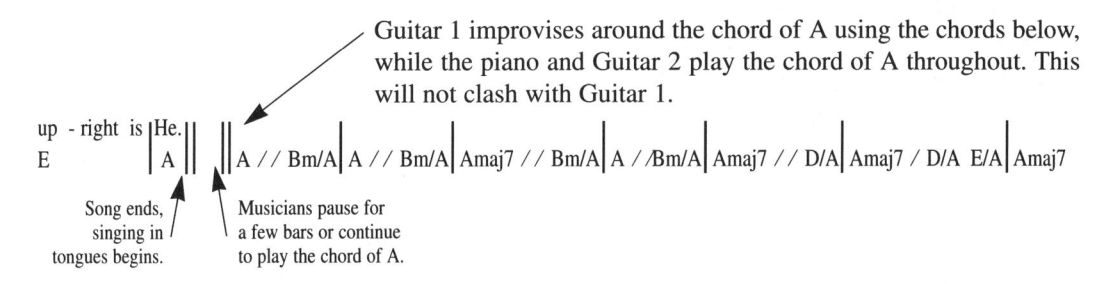

Guitar 1 improvises around the chord of A using the chords below, while the piano and Guitar 2 play the chord of A throughout. This will not clash with Guitar 1.

up - right is |He.‖ ‖
E | A ‖   ‖ A // Bm/A | A // Bm/A | Amaj7 // Bm/A | A //Bm/A | Amaj7 // D/A | Amaj7 / D/A E/A | Amaj7

Song ends,   Musicians pause for
singing in   a few bars or continue
tongues begins.   to play the chord of A.

Below are the chords for the previous example and their equivalents in other easy keys. *Note:* the circled numbers refer to the frets. (The nut = 0.)

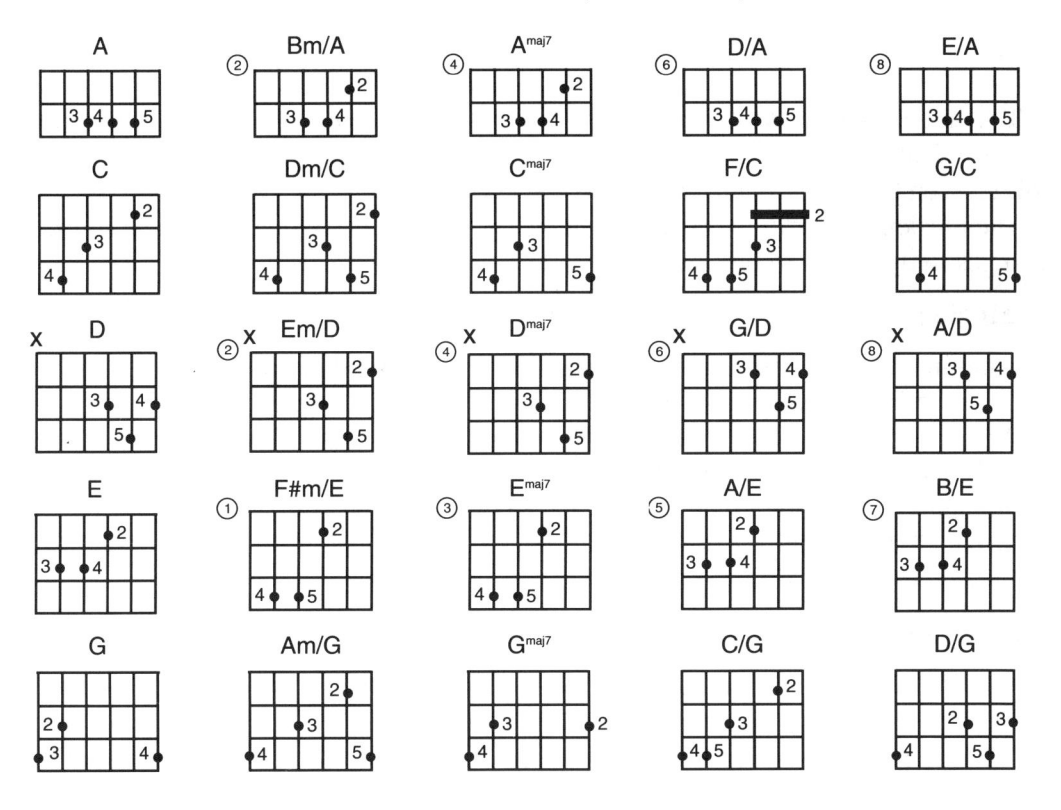

A   Bm/A ②   A^maj7 ④   D/A ⑥   E/A ⑧

C   Dm/C   C^maj7   F/C   G/C

x D   x Em/D ②   x D^maj7 ④   x G/D ⑥   x A/D ⑧

E   F#m/E ①   E^maj7 ③   A/E ⑤   B/E ⑦

G   Am/G   G^maj7   C/G   D/G

79

(c) Play a sequence (a few chords repeated) with a rhythm

See the table of chord sequences on page 75 for further ideas.

The repetitious nature of a sequence can provide a secure framework for people to sing in the Spirit. For many, launching out into a new language can be enough of a problem without having to compose melodies as well.

In rehearsals, the musicians should be planning to use these sequences after particular songs (maybe a couple at the most). In the meeting, it may suddenly not feel right to use what has been prepared but at least the musicians are prepared.

As the chief musician establishes the sequential phrase, the other musicians must be sensitive to the leader getting louder, softer, slowing down or injecting more rhythm. The leader must make the accents very clear.

Keep the chords in the sequence simple, otherwise this will distract an already worshipping congregation; any creativity should aim to serve, not take over worship.

For example, *Emmanuel* (SoF 83)

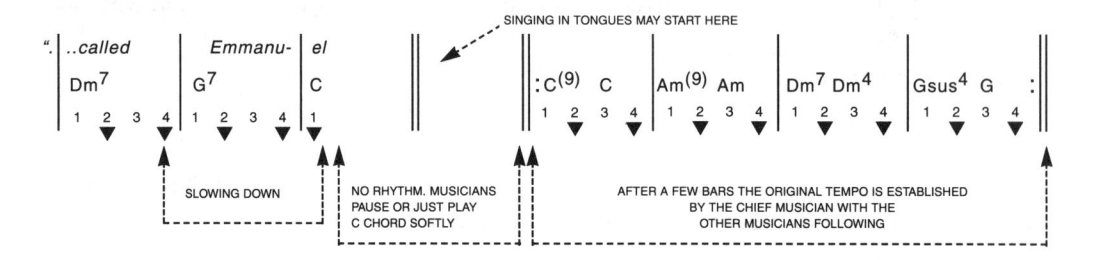

The above points can be played in different ways. Either (i) softly throughout, (ii) gradually growing in volume (crescendo) then dying away (decrescendo), (iii) crescendo, decrescendo, crescendo, decrescendo.

The musicians need to work at the chemistry and sensitivity between them for these changes in dynamics to be smooth.

3. Singing in tongues – out of a time of quiet

Singing in tongues can be especially beautiful when started out of a period of stillness and silence in the meeting. As people are quiet, sensing the presence of God in their midst, you could say, 'Let's be quietly singing in tongues, focusing our minds on the Lord.' I have found this approach especially helpful in encouraging many to take their first tentative steps along what can appear to be a spiritual gang-plank.

Note: All the possibilities and various dynamic combinations in sections 1 and 2 can be used in this third section.

Worship or the worship of worship?

Obviously great attention needs to be paid to what is happening in the congregation when these suggestions are carried out. The musicians must be careful that they don't rush ahead and try to carry the congregation further than they are ready to go. If the musicians are concentrating on *serving* the congregation and the Lord with their music, it will help guard against the subtle, inconspicuous ways in which self-indulgence and ego-projecting can creep into the worship. Worship which becomes 'gimmicky' will not set us free but will have quite the opposite effect. Just because there is an absence of liturgy and form doesn't mean worship is being produced. Often when the desire to worship is at its strongest, it is then that we need to make sure that it is being directed to God alone. When we are at our most creative in worship, self-gratification may well be close to the surface. Therefore, we need to *be* worshippers and not *do* worship.

PART THREE
Leading Worship

11. *The Worship Leader*

The worship leader is both a *worshipper* and a *leader*.

1. As worshipper

We minister not by what we *do* but by what we *are*. This is what sounds out above the noise of our music and chatter of our words. God wants our worship to be living and our living to be worship. If our worship is event-orientated, we will always feel self-conscious. If the only time you ever worship with your instrument is in public, you will find it hard to lead others. If you haven't got measles, you won't infect anyone!

Worship flows out of relationships.

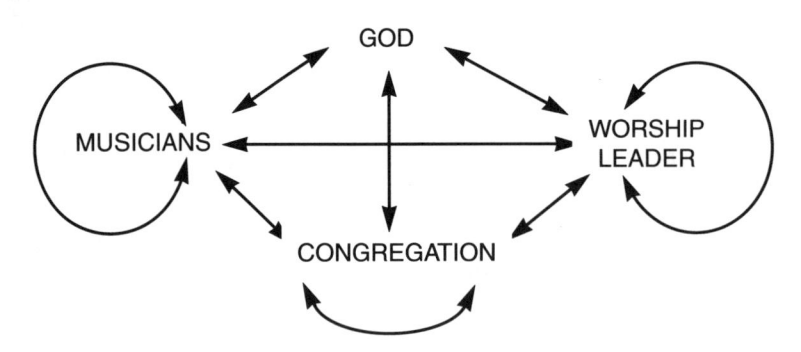

```
              GOD
               ↕
    MUSICIANS ↔ ↔ WORSHIP LEADER
               ↕
          CONGREGATION
```

To lead effectively you must be secure in your relationship in five areas.

(a) Yourself

Have a healthy self-acceptance. You can't have for others what you haven't got for yourself.

Personal confidence is essential. This comes from an inner conviction of God's calling which sustains us through difficult times. Over-confidence is as bad as a lack of confidence.

Don't project self-doubts. Don't read into situations things which don't exist. The sighting of a stony face in the congregation can easily be taken personally, when actually the person might simply have a headache.

Don't respond to any 'negative static' you might be picking up. Don't get drawn into vindicating yourself. Leave that to God.

Don't be over-defensive about your ministry. Defensiveness is a sign of owning and possessing. Remember, we are partakers in Christ's ministry.

(b) God

His love. You can't bring others further than you've been yourself.

His forgiveness. Unless you've appreciated what God has done for you, you might use your position to elevate yourself.

His holiness. Howard Hendricks once said, 'If your Christianity doesn't work at home, it doesn't work – don't try to export it!' Before you can be a man before men, you must be a man before God.

His voice. Be able to discern his direction, otherwise leading will simply mean neatly linking a few songs together. An ambassador who speaks for the king must be in constant touch with the throne. Don't lead on your own.

His ministry. Don't try to gauge the Spirit's work in the meeting. He always does more than we see. Especially when we are tired or unwell, we may think, 'I didn't feel the worship went well, therefore it didn't.'

(c) The leader (minister, vicar, pastor)

Don't misuse the trust placed in you. The tail shouldn't wag the dog! Sometimes the tail isn't even connected to the dog!

Don't over-run the time allotted to you unless you are permitted to do so. 'Well, I just felt led!' is usually an indication that the worship leader is suffering from 'led-poisoning'.

Don't speak harshly to the people. Leave any admonishing to the leader. Know where your responsibilities begin and end.

Have comeback after the meeting. There may be limitations in evaluating what God did but we can assess what we did and improve on it.

(d) The musicians (this includes the PA and OHP operator)

In a sense, the whole group is the worship leader. The chief musician is the co-ordinator.

The leader's aim must be to further the spiritual and musical development of the team around him or her. There must be a good rapport between them. The emphasis should be on enjoying togetherness rather than getting things right.

Don't correct anyone within earshot of the congregation immediately after the meeting. Discuss how things went at a later date when you are all less tired and therefore more receptive.

Pray together immediately after the meeting. The same applies if only one person has been leading. Let's spiritually guard each other's backs.

(e) The people

When leading, you are pastoring. You have to know where the people are. It's no good singing songs of triumph when many people are hurting.

Identify with them. Avoid using 'you'. Use 'we'. This helps to stress togetherness.

Don't drive the people. Draw them. Realise that you can't draw out worship that isn't there.

Don't scold. You naturally have more expectation than them since you have prayed, practised and prepared yourself. You might want the people to be where you are but God accepts them where they are. People may have little expectation because life has knocked them around lately.

Avoid the traffic warden mentality, where you are on the look-out to book members of the reluctant minority.

Don't go at the rate of the slowest. If you do, you won't go anywhere because they're likely to have their heels dug in!

Encourage individuals who pray, exercise a spiritual gift, or give a testimony, to speak up. Where appropriate, repeat a paraphrased version of it if you sense that many couldn't hear.

2. As leader

(a) Negatives

People need to feel secure – a worship leader has to grant them this security. Having said that, there will be times when we have to cope with our negative feelings. Like a swan we might be calm and serene on the surface but paddling like mad underneath!

(b) Nerves.

Don't expect not to be nervous. Do expect not to be afraid. 'Perfect love casts out all fear'. I wonder whether this includes nerves as well?! If the nerves are a problem repeatedly, don't bottle it up. Talk it out with someone in leadership. There should be someone appointed for pastoral oversight of the musicians and worship leaders. Before leading, think of an introductory sentence.

(c) Expressiveness.

You can't expect the people to be expressive if you're not. Worship leaders are the model. We set the tone. We have to be what we want the people to be. This also applies to being expectant as a leadership team.

(d) Security.

The team leading the meeting need to be clear about what they're after under God for that meeting. For instance, if the worship leader hasn't got a firm sense of direction before the meeting, the congregation can end up dictating what should happen. Your instructions beforehand are the rock on which you stand. Even if the tone you set is initially met with flatness, don't be intimidated by the attitude of the congregation. It might be that you are shifting the majority of them from a wrong focus.

(e) Body language

Some worship leaders can inadvertently draw people's attention away from the Lord to themselves. In the light of this, here are some points to take note of.

(i) Manner. Don't assume a sophisticated or 'religious' air. Don't speak in an affected tone of voice. Musicians, especially trained ones, should remember they are there to

establish a platform for someone else! They are to be like a signpost which is in a prominent position but pointing away from itself. It's good to have good musicians but you don't have to be one to lead worship.

(ii) Body. Stand in a relaxed, friendly posture, conveying a sense of purpose and authority. Two extremes to be avoided are slouching or standing to attention. Don't stand woodenly or hide behind a music stand. Respond (or encourage the members of the group not holding or playing instruments to respond) with the appropriate gestures, eg, hands raised, kneeling, bowing, etc.

(iii) Face. Don't allow the microphone to obstruct the congregation's view of your face. Don't be smile-proof! Sometimes we may have to be like the stewardess on the aeroplane, being cordial despite the difficulties she's experiencing with certain passengers. Sometimes we may have to cover for each other in taking the strain.

(iv) Hands. Don't play with the microphone while talking.

(v) Eyes. Establish sight lines to the following:

(a) The main leader of the meeting. Don't lead with your eyes closed. You have the rest of the week to do that. The leader of the meeting, to whom you are accountable, can't catch your attention if you're lost in wonder, love and oblivion.
(b) The congregation. They see you one-to-one. Your tendency will be to see them as a blob. So regard them as individuals. Look at them. Don't avoid eye-contact.
Don't pay attention to distractions such as latecomers or someone going to the toilet. If you do, everyone else will.
(c) Musicians. Instil confidence in them. If you are likely to repeat a chorus section, don't announce this half a second before the chorus. Any directions need to be reinforced with hand movements or, if you are a guitarist, with facial expressions!

(vi) Voice. Learn how to say very little! Worship leaders generally say too much. Avoid jargon. Are we the same outside ministry, when we take our worship leader's or musician's hat off?

Give a non-religious explanation for certain things occurring in the meeting, eg, tongues.

Let your enthusiasm be reflected in your voice. Modulate it according to what you're saying, either soft or exultant.

Keep your mouth roughly two inches away and two inches above the microphone. Don't mumble. Speak up – always speak to the people in the back row – and speak slowly. We tend to speak faster when nervous.

Express your ideas with an economy of words. Use (a) Biblical imagery, eg, Isaiah 40:11-12: 'He will feed his flock like a shepherd. He will gather his lambs in his arms. He will carry them in his bosom and gently lead them…' and (b) Illustrations, eg, 'God is more willing to forgive you than a father is willing to pluck his child from a fire.'

Keep it brief. Remember, you are not a Bible expositor. God's anointing is on the music.

(vii) Distracting mannerisms. Ask yourself, or even someone else, whether you have any irritating habits which cause people's stress level to rise. Do you help people to unwind or do you wind them up?

Conclusion

The main attributes of a good worship leader are:

> ANOINTING – ABILITY – AUTHORITY

or to put it another way:

> SANCTIFICATION – SUBMISSION – SENSITIVITY – SKILL

12. The Meeting

Authority and accountability

The following diagram may help you get an overview of people's responsibilities and authority/accountability for a meeting.

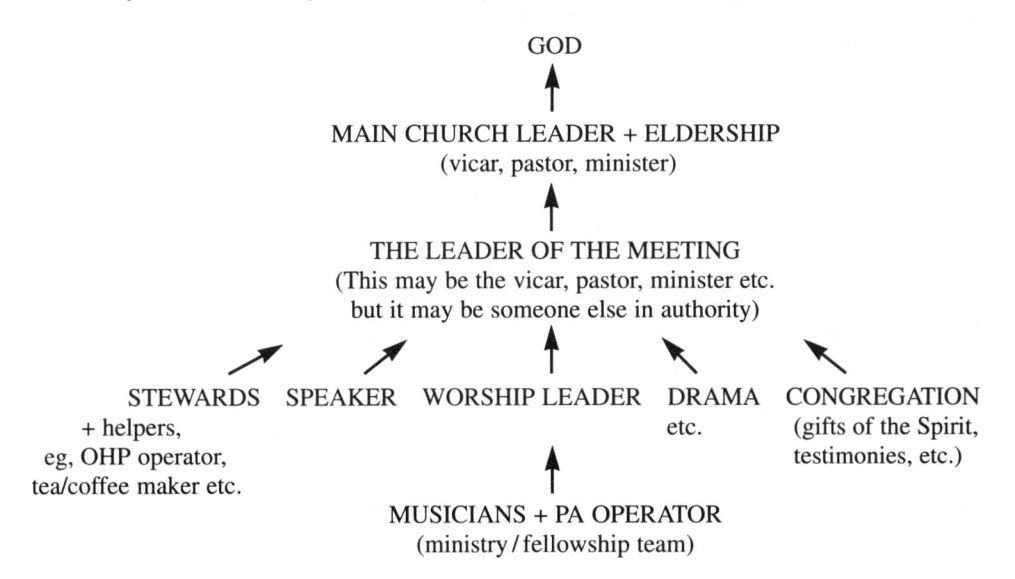

```
                              GOD
                               ↑
                               |
                MAIN CHURCH LEADER + ELDERSHIP
                    (vicar, pastor, minister)
                               ↑
                               |
                   THE LEADER OF THE MEETING
              (This may be the vicar, pastor, minister etc.
                but it may be someone else in authority)
             ↗       ↗          ↑         ↖          ↖
      STEWARDS   SPEAKER   WORSHIP LEADER  DRAMA   CONGREGATION
      + helpers,                            etc.   (gifts of the Spirit,
    eg, OHP operator,                              testimonies, etc.)
    tea/coffee maker etc.          ↑
                                   |
                       MUSICIANS + PA OPERATOR
                       (ministry / fellowship team)
```

Before the meeting, the worship leader must clarify with the leader of the meeting and the speaker what the theme is. The worship leader can then prepare the songs for the worship and bring those to rehearsals with the musicians and PA team. The worship leader and musicians should have someone such as an elder whose role it is to pastor them. This shields the main church leader from always having to deal with every grievance. If the worship leader is not a musician, he should not simply give the list of songs to the chief musician for the rehearsal but should attend in person.

Before each meeting, a team of prayers should be covering the meeting and the musicians' sound-checking for it. There may not be time for the worship leader, musicians and leader of the meeting to be in for the whole of this prayer meeting but there should be some prayer together as well as a final clarifying of the order and times allowed.

When everyone is connected and submitted to one another, the full potential of God's magnetic presence can draw us to himself. As with any magnet, the individual metal particles become as magnetic as the magnet itself.

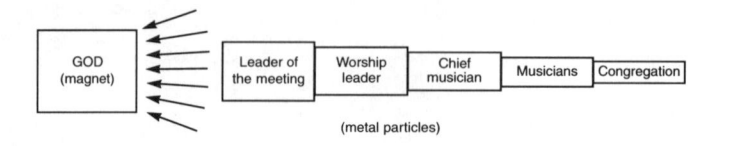

```
  GOD         Leader of   Worship   Chief       Musicians  Congregation
(magnet)     the meeting   leader   musician
                          (metal particles)
```

Lift off

Here are some points to bear in mind as the meeting commences.

1. Teach any new songs at the beginning

The worship experience is like a dance. It is hard to enjoy dancing while you are still concentrating on the steps. Similarly, a song may not go very well at first not because people don't like the song, but because they are still focused on the mechanics of singing.

2. Continue with the rest of the meeting

Try not to use songs as polyfilla between other elements of the meeting, eg, hymns, reading, etc. This can cause the meeting to lurch along. Have a block time of worship. Apart from avoiding any unnecessary breaks, the music acts as a bridge to help us to move from self-consciousness to God-consciousness.

The Hebrews understood that moving into the presence of God was done by degrees. The Psalms of Ascent (120-134) were sung on feast days, journeying into Jerusalem. They show a people moving from an awareness of their problems to an awareness of God's presence, starting with petitioning God and ending in blessing God.

At the same time, people must bear in mind that they shouldn't use half the worship time to warm up. Instead of worship being a selfless act it can become quite the opposite, where members of a congregation come with their empty spiritual buckets, expecting the worship leader to fill them. Our main ministry in life is to minister to God (1 Chron 15:2; 16:4; 16:37; 2 Chron 29:11; Ezek 44:15). Without the understanding that God experiences pleasure (Rev 4:11) as we worship him, the focus of our meetings will centre on us.

3. Pray

Like a champagne bottle being broken at a ship's launch, or a gun being fired at the start of a race, this prayer should signal the commencement of a time of meaning business with God. You could ask a few people to pray briefly, so that right at the beginning the congregation are being involved in taking ownership for the success of the meeting.

4. Say very little

The worship leader is not there to preach sermons, not even short ones. A simple seed-thought is ample. The longer you speak the less focused people will be. Don't frustrate a congregation which is ready to worship with irrelevant truths, however noble.

5. Tell the people to stand

The quality and volume of singing is often improved when people are standing. It also aids concentration. State it graciously, don't suggest it timidly. Say that as the worship continues, they should feel free to sit, stand, kneel, or (where appropriate) lie prostrate before the Lord.

6. Instrumental introductions

These should be:

(a) Played by one person. This saves having to count-in for the group. It also avoids the dissonance sometimes created by one musician playing A–D–E and another playing A–E–D.

(b) Rehearsed. As part of making people feel they are in capable hands, have well-defined introductions, so that no one is left in doubt as to when the introduction is over and when they are required to sing.

(c) Brief. They should be either four or eight bars in length.

(d) Well accented. A common unsettling occurrence is when a musician plays the opening chord and immediately starts singing, expecting everyone to sing in time. Set a regular pulse which prepares people to sing together. Musicians should emphasise the accents clearly in the introductions.

(e) Confident. If the introduction is played timidly, the singing is likely to begin in a similar fashion. Start as you mean to go on.

(f) Not slowing down. Part of the aim of the introduction is to set a tempo for everyone to sing in time with. If you then slow down, the original tempo has to be restated. The solution to helping people know where the introduction ends and where the singing starts is to increase the volume, not slow the tempo of the strumming.

Introduction to songs (a simplified approach)

(i) Which chords to use for an introduction. These are best based around the chords of I, IV, and V. The table below should be self explanatory.

The key in which the song is based	*I	II	III	*IV	*V	VI	VII
A	*A	B	C#	*D	E	F#	G
B♭ (A#)	*B♭	C	D	*E♭	*F	G	A♭
B	*B	C#	D#	*E	*F#	G#	A#
C	*C	D	E	*F	*G	A	B
D♭ (C#)	*D♭	E♭	F	*G♭	*A♭	B♭	C
D	*D	E	F#	*G	*A	B	C#
E♭ (D#)	*E♭	F	G	*A♭	*B♭	C	D
E	*E	F#	G#	*A	*B	C#	D#
F	*F	G	A	*B♭	*C	D	E
G♭ (F#)	*G♭	A♭	B♭	*B	*D♭	E♭	F

Example: Song in key of A – Intro: A(I), D(IV) and E(V).

Example: Song in key of Am – Intro: Am(Im), Dm(IVm) and E(V).

Note: For *minor* keys, remember that I and IV are *minor* chords and V is *major*.

(ii) The format of an introduction. Lay your introductions out like this: (Cassette example 65)

```
         1 bar           ½ bar ½ bar   REPEAT
       ┌─────────┐     ┌─────┬─────┐
       │ A(I)    │     │D(IV)│E(V) │   A(I)         D(IV)    E(V)
       │1+2+3+4+ │     │1+2+3+4+   │   1+2+3+4+     1+2+3+4+
       │ ▼   ▼   │     │ ▼    ▼    │   ▼   ▼        ▼▼▼▼▼ ▼
                                                    All down strokes
```

Increase volume
(This alerts people to get ready to sing, rather than if you made no rhythmic indication).

This system of I–IV–V is used for all the introductions to songs in this book.

7. Lead the singing in

The first phrase of a song needs to be sung with greater clarity than the rest of the song. Don't leave the congregation in doubt. Sing the melody rather than trying harmonies. If you do like to use harmonies, make sure other singers are carrying the main melody.

Just a note on song-selection criteria at this point: the first song should not be too high in range, otherwise people might begin to resist the worship process. Let their voices get warmed up first before you choose songs that are using lots of top Cs and Ds.

Your aim at the outset is to rally the people together and to create a sense of oneness before moving on.

8. Singing and playing simultaneously

If you find the combination of singing and maintaining steady accents difficult, at least try to sing the first phrase of each important section of the song and then return to concentrate on your playing. If you don't at least do this, people will not be clear merely from your instrumental introduction where they are supposed to come in.

Keep the strumming simple. The main feature of strumming should be its *regular accents*, so you can afford to edit strumming to its bare essentials.

9. Speaking and playing simultaneously

Learn how to give instructions between verses, such as, 'just voices'; 'the last verse again'; etc, without losing tempo or playing wrong chords. This needs practice. Isolate such areas and become fluent in them. Speak with extra clarity and volume, leaving no one in doubt, making the phrase fit in.

Practise this in a song, first going back to the beginning and secondly going back to the chorus. So in a song such as *Father God* your first announcement would be 'Father God' and your second would be 'I will sing'. (Cassette example 66)

```
     B7        | Em       "Father God" | Em
     for ever- | more.                  | Father God ...
       ▼          ▼          ▼   ▼        ▼
       3   4    | 1    2    3    4      | 1    2

     B7        | Em       "I will sing" | Em
     for ever- | more.                  | I will sing ...
       ▼          ▼          ▼▼▼▼         ▼
       3   4    | 1    2    3    4      | 1    2
```

(You don't have to sing 'for ever more'. This might feel strange to you but the singing of the congregation will mask your sudden absence.)

Announcements should not be rushed, so you need to leave plenty of space to give them extra clarity.

After the announcement, lead the singing back in confidently.

10. Keep the worship flowing

You can break the flow with too much talking, and introductions to songs can become like adverts during a film. 'Guard your steps when you go to the house of God … let your words be few' (Eccles 5:1-2).

To avoid the worship becoming stilted after each song, let the musicians continue to play very softly on one chord or sequence (a few chords) as illustrated below.

Note: The technique of laying down a soft carpet of music between songs is best suited to quieter worship rather than lively praise.

Example:

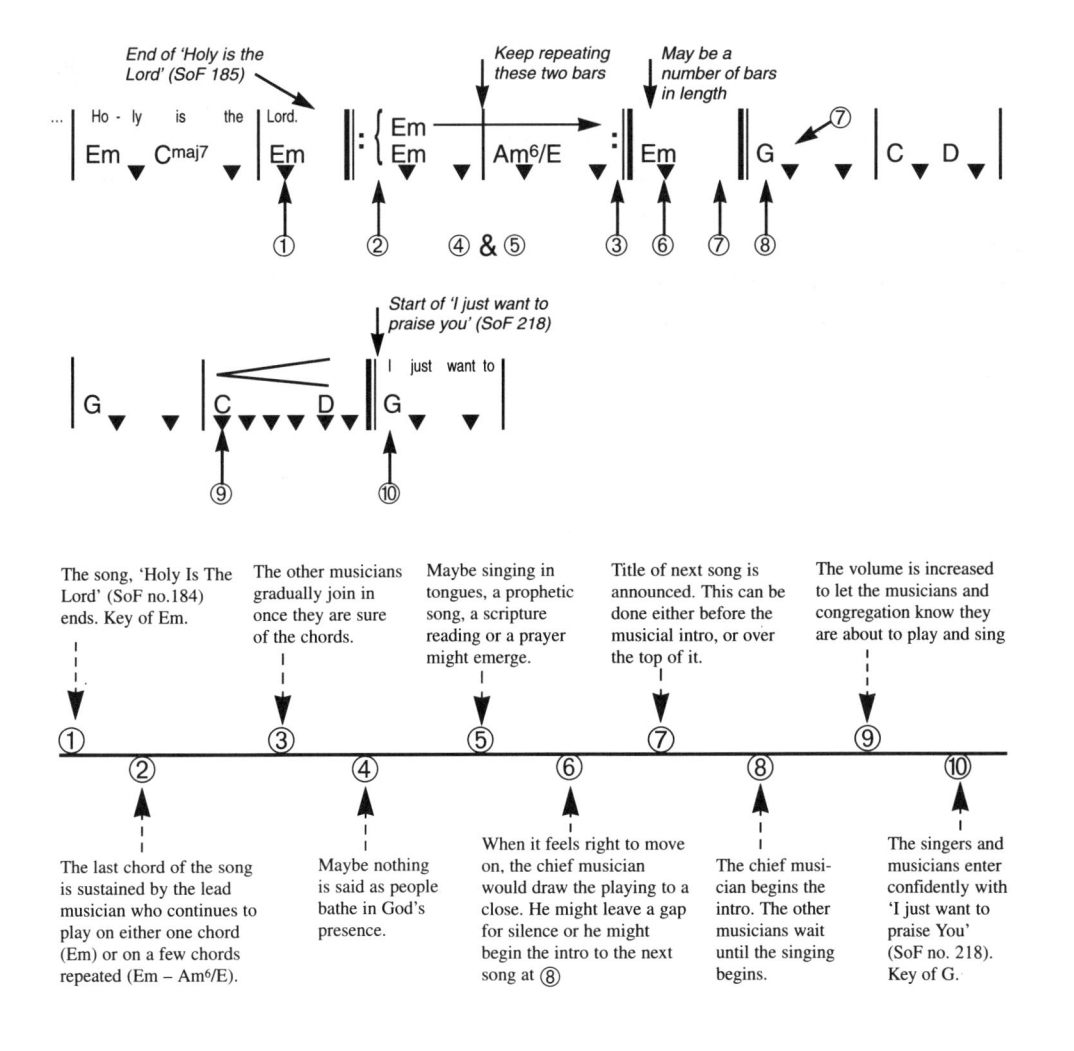

The worship experience is like a journey. As on any journey, most of the fuel and energy is consumed in stopping and starting. The process described above can help to smooth out the wrinkles.

Try to become comfortable with different types of songs. Some leaders cause the worship to be predictable because of their preference for one style of music. For example, non-rhythmic or up-tempo. You are not there to play your favourites.

Avoid abrupt changes in tempo or theme. Don't alternate between lively and slow songs or between thanksgiving, warfare and adoration. Know what God is emphasising in your fellowship at present and teach songs which reinforce that. Know the 'season' your church is in.

You don't have to sing *all* the songs you've rehearsed. One song might become the 'kingpin' of the meeting. God might want you to dwell on a particular song, singing it repeatedly, until people appear to be coming into the realisation of its message. Meaningful repetition can help the truths to penetrate further and further into us, until our spirit is coated with them. In this way, we are not just singing words but absorbing their meaning. Unless worship changes us, it's not worship.

God is our friend. When we communicate with a true friend, our concentration is not on the dynamics of relating. We are just getting on together. Similarly, when we worship God, our attention should not be on the mechanics of communication, eg, hands raised, etc, but on the fact that we are simply sharing an experience with God. Worship means to simply love God and to love him simply.

When two friends meet, the appropriate exchanges are, 'Hi! How are you?' It would be rather worrying if after half an hour they were still talking about the weather! So in worship too, God wants us to move deeper with him.

Without this expectation that the Father seeks worshippers (Jn 4:23), that he is wanting to come near and draw us to himself, leaders can construct the format of a meeting round God's *absence* rather than his *presence*. The result is that songs are used as a means of 'getting the people going' or quietening them down. Worship becomes technique- and formula-based, rather than us relating to God and God relating back. For him to respond seems very natural. This is the basis of all relationships. It dishonours him to think that he wouldn't want to interact with us.

PART FOUR
Creativity in Worship

13. *Improving Your Worship Expression*

Variety – the spice of life

The following ideas have no spiritual value in themselves, they are merely aids to worship. They are not to be used for their own sake, as tricks up your sleeve or as ornamental extras, but rather as an integral part of your worship expression. Though they can help to prevent songs becoming dull and predictable and guard against mindless repetition, their main purpose is to state the message of the song more skilfully – underscoring, heightening and creating a deeper awareness of the meaning of the words, so that they have a greater impact on the singer. A new perspective can be given on well-worn songs.

There is little value in using my ideas in parrot fashion. They are to be adapted for use with your own repertoire. Plan thoughtfully the use of these techniques prior to the worship. Be careful not to program your songs (eg, second time – just instruments; third time – just voices, etc). Each idea must be a response to the worship at a given moment. Creativity must issue from an encounter with God.

If you are leading worship where few, if any, of the following variations have ever been used, don't suddenly incorporate them without first preparing the people. At the beginning of the worship you could say that there are many and various ways in which we can worship God (list a few of these ideas) and conclude by saying that these are a small reflection of the variety and creativity of our God.

Instructions for leaders and musicians

In the gap between one verse and the next, the musicians should drop the volume of their playing slightly so that they and the congregation can hear the leader's instructions (eg, 'Just the instruments.'). This can be done as follows:
   Guitarists – play half as many strokes (but still maintain the accents).
   Keyboards – play half as many notes (chords of longer length).
   Woodwind, brass, strings – stop playing.
   Drums – stop playing quavers on the high-hat (but still maintain the beat).
Note: The following occur after the song has been sung a few times through.

1. Just the ladies

Instructing the ladies to sing while the men wait their turn can have the feel of a choir practice. Therefore, this technique must be used sparingly and meaningfully. If you instruct the ladies to sing a verse, don't automatically give the next verse to the men. Choose which songs would benefit most from this idea.

Example: Jesus, how lovely You are (SoF 287). Just the ladies sing, 'Hallelujah! Jesus is pure and holy …' The rest of the song is to be sung by everyone.

2. Just the men

The use of any idea is to enhance the words. Never instruct *just* the ladies or *just* the men to sing simply because you fear it might be tedious for them to sing it a number of times together.

Example: Isn't He beautiful (SoF 250). Have the men sing it once through, without the ladies doing the same. In an age where men often find it difficult to articulate the way they feel, encouraging the men alone to sing of the effect of the love of Jesus on their hearts and emotions can have great power. Indeed, at the end of one conference, someone told me that out of all the talks, seminars and times of worship, this had touched him the most.

3. First the ladies, then the men (or vice versa)

Example: Worthy art Thou (SoF 614). 'Worthy art Thou, O Lord our God' (L); 'For You are reigning…' (M); 'Jesus is Lord of all the earth' (T).

Example: Rejoice! (SoF 480). 'God is at work in us' (L); 'Where things impossible' (M); 'Rejoice!' (T). (M = men, L = ladies, T = together.)

4. Changing the words

In the title. Constantly review your repertoire to see whether there is some way you can bring freshness to what may have become over-familiar words.

For example, change the words of the song *Jesus, Your love has melted my heart* to 'Jesus, Your love *is* melting my heart.' There are always going to be people in a meeting for whom the words 'has melted' are simply not true. It might be best to start by singing 'is melting'. Before the song, you might even say, 'Let's allow the Spirit to come and thaw out those stony areas of our lives where we are hard of heart and touchy.' Then, as you come to the last time through, you could announce, 'Your love *has* melted my heart.' The musicians could reflect this change in words by raising the volume of their playing.

I was in a prayer meeting where a lady asked for prayer because a certain relationship difficulty had brought her to the very brink of abandoning her faith in God. As we prayed for her, we sensed the Lord wanted to refresh her tired spirit. As part of our prayer, we sang *River, wash over me* (SoF 487), changing the word 'me' to her name. This song could also be used when praying about situations where there is national or domestic unrest.

In the verse or chorus. For example, *Worthy art Thou* (SoF 614). Change the words of the chorus, 'Jesus is Lord of all the earth,' to, 'Jesus is Lord of all my life.' Or in *When the Spirit of the Lord* (SoF 598), as well as 'sing', 'clap', 'praise' and 'dance' you could insert 'shout' and 'leap'. Also, a whole verse can be sung to 'la'.

5. In the singular and plural

In the song *He is Lord* (SoF 165), you could sing differently on each verse: 'He's our Lord'; 'You're my Lord'; 'You're our Lord'. You could vary it even further by omitting the accompaniment or playing it very softly when you come to sing, 'You're my Lord.' Apart from adding contrast, it would give a more personal, private touch. (Remember that as you come to that particular verse, you would have to announce, '"You're *my* Lord" – softly,' so that people capture the spirit in which it is to be sung.)

6. Just the guitar

There are incidents in the Scriptures where instrumental music clearly ministered to people. When King Saul was being tormented by an evil spirit (in 1 Samuel 15–23), the remedy for his oppression was a curious one. David was summoned to Saul's court, not to *pray* but to *play*. We are told that whenever David played his lyre the evil spirit left Saul, and he was refreshed. So, the incident occurred more than once. Therefore, it was not coincidental. We have to ask ourselves what God might be saying to us through such a passage and how we should act on the implications.

7. Just the voices

This technique is best used with songs where your fellowship seems to naturally use harmonies. It isn't so effective with melodies sung in unison. Harmonisation is a wonderful picture of varieties of gifts working together to a common goal. The overall effect should be of different vocal lines weaving together a kind of musical tapestry. In order to prevent people feeling that the bottom of the song has suddenly dropped out, you will have to take a firmer grip on leading the song at that point, especially on the first phrase. To encourage people to launch out into singing harmonies and descants, begin singing this verse with a harmony line yourself.

Example: I love You, Lord (SoF 226).

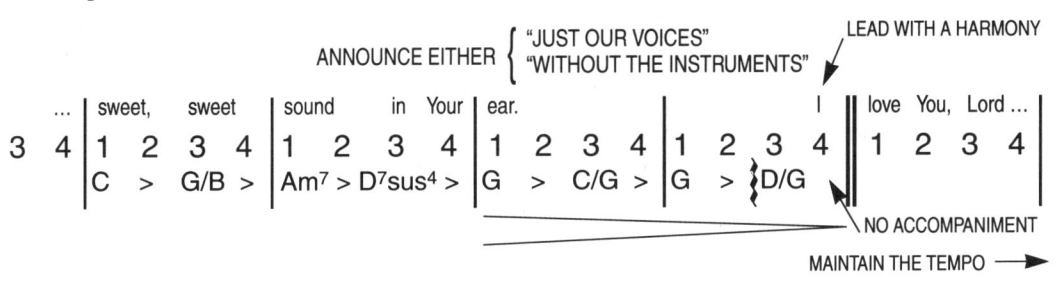

```
                              ┌ "JUST OUR VOICES"           LEAD WITH A HARMONY
             ANNOUNCE EITHER ─┤                                   ↙
                              └ "WITHOUT THE INSTRUMENTS" ↙
     ... │ sweet,  sweet  │ sound   in Your │ ear.    │            │ ║ love You, Lord ... │
  3   4  │ 1   2   3   4  │ 1   2   3   4   │ 1  2  3  4 │ 1  2  3  4 ║ 1   2   3   4
         │ C   >   G/B  > │ Am⁷ > D⁷sus⁴ >  │ G  > C/G > │ G  > {D/G
                                                                    ↘ NO ACCOMPANIMENT
                                                                      MAINTAIN THE TEMPO ⟶
```

Important notes

(a) As you make the announcement for voices only, drop the volume of your playing.

(b) Lead the singing with a harmony.

(c) Since there is no instrumental accompaniment on the vocal verse, there will be a tendency for the tempo to drag. If this is only slight, it can be quite effective, but you need to beware of its becoming too much like a dirge.

(d) It can be quite effective for this unaccompanied vocal verse to be the last verse of the song.

(e) If you are going to sing another verse with accompaniment, lead the singing in clearly (not a harmony line).

8. First the guitar, then voices

This variation can be applied to any song which has two contrasting sections. For example: SoF nos 1, 43, 111, 151, 192, 209, 268, 287, 290, 325, 541, 614, 627, 115, 144, 152, 266, 379, 493, 554.

Example: Father God (SoF 92). Musicians play the section, 'Father God, I wonder....' The congregation join in at, 'I will sing Your praises....' The leader would have to say, 'I will sing...' the bar before that section, which would mean leaving out the last phrase of the verse ('you're there to guide me') to fit it in.

9. Humming

This is best done with songs that are: (a) worshipful and meditative; (b) not up-tempo; (c) pitched in the middle-range for voice; (d) not too lengthy.

Songs such as *Within the veil* would be suitable, but songs such as *I will enter His gates* should be avoided – unless you want to run the risk of people bursting blood vessels! In the gap before the verse where the humming will take place, announce, 'Let's hum the tune.' Don't just say, 'Hum.'

Some people find that singing 'ooh' is more comfortable than humming. To facilitate this, as you lead alternate between humming and oohing, so that others can follow.

The musicians should play very softly while people hum. Particular instruments may have to stop playing to re-enter in the next verse.

10. Contrasting sections

By creating areas of light and shade in a song, we can heighten the words so that people see them very differently. For example, in *Jesus, how lovely You are* (SoF 287), play the choruses softly and the verses loudly (except the verse beginning, 'Hallelujah! Jesus is meek and lowly....' Capture the sentiment of the words by playing it *softly*). This is far better than the whole song being played at one volume. You could also strum the choruses and verses differently. The accents on the choruses could be on 2 and 4 whereas the strumming on the verses could be on 1, 2, 3 and 4 (as shown in the following diagram). In the gaps between choruses and verses, I woud suggest you lead it as follows:

```
                        "HALLELUJAH"
       ... how | lovely You are.    ‖ Hal - le - lu - jah! | Je - sus is ...
        3   4  | 1   2   3   4      ‖ 1   2   3   4        | 1   2   3
               | G7      C          ‖ C           F        | G
               |     >   > > >      ‖ >   >   >   >        | >   >   >
```

Also in *I will call upon the Lord* (SoF 266):
Section 1: 'I will call upon the Lord…' (half-tempo);
Section 2: 'The Lord liveth…' (double-time).

```
SECTION 1                                    SECTION 2
| so   shall  I    be | saved from my ene - mies. The‖ Lord       liv-eth    and | blessed be my rock…
| 1    2     3    4  | 1     2      3       4         ‖ 1 + 2 + 3 + 4 +           | 1 + 2 + 3 +
| D         C     G  | D            C       G         ‖ D                         | G         D
|    >         >     |       >             >          ‖   >   >   >   >           |   >     >   >
```

⟵ Notice the change ⟶
in accents

11. Highlighting particular lines

For example in *I love You, Lord* (SoF 226).

```
                                         "I | love you, Lord    | and I lift    my |
‖ G     C/G   | G     D/G   | G     C/G       | G     D/G        |
  1  2  3  4  | 1  2  3  4  | 1  2  3  4      | 1  2  3  4       |
     >     >    > > > > > >      >     >           >      >
```

"LET'S LIFT OUR VOICES!"
```
| voice              |            To  | wor - ship    | you.    O    my |
| G     C/G   | G     G⁷    | C     G/B     | Am     G       |
  1  2  3  4 | 1  2  3  4  | 1  2  3  4    | 1  2  3  4     |
     >     >    > > > > > >      >     >        >     >
```

{ "TAKE JOY!"
{ "REJOICE!"
```
| soul,      re- | joice.    Take | joy my King   | in what you…" |
| D     D/C  | G/B   D/A   | G     C/G     | G     D/G     |
  1  2  3  4 | 1  2  3  4  | 1  2  3  4    | 1  2  3  4    |
     >     >   >   > > > >      >     >        >     >
```

Here, the phrases 'lift my voice', 'O my soul, rejoice!' and 'take joy my King' are being highlighted. It would not be advisable to make this many announcements in one verse. (You're a worship leader not a bingo caller!) I've done it this way to show you the various possibilities.

12. Different tempos in a song

With careful and positive vocal and instrumental leading, a worship leader can further colour the fabric of a song by introducing different tempos. For example, in *Thank You, Jesus* (SoF 523):

Verse 1 (Thank You, Jesus): usual version played up-tempo and loud.
Verse 2 (You went to Calvary): usual version played up-tempo and moderately loud.
Verse 3 (You rose up from the grave): usual version, up-tempo and loud.

Verse 4 (You went to Calvary): new arrangement, slow and soft. Possibly sing twice through.
Verse 5 (You rose up from the grave): usual version, up-tempo and loud.
Verse 6 (Thank You, Jesus): usual version, up-tempo and very loud.

The aim of changing tempo in a song is to dramatise the words. After singing this song, one person confessed that the truth of such conventional yet profound Christian statements as, 'You went to Calvary' and 'You rose up from the grave' hit him forcibly.

Execution: In terms of the mechanics of leading such an arrangement the problem areas are likely to come when setting new tempos. (In this example, between verses 3 and 4, 5 and 6.) This needs to be led clearly and confidently.

Here is the end of the fourth verse leading into the new arrangement.

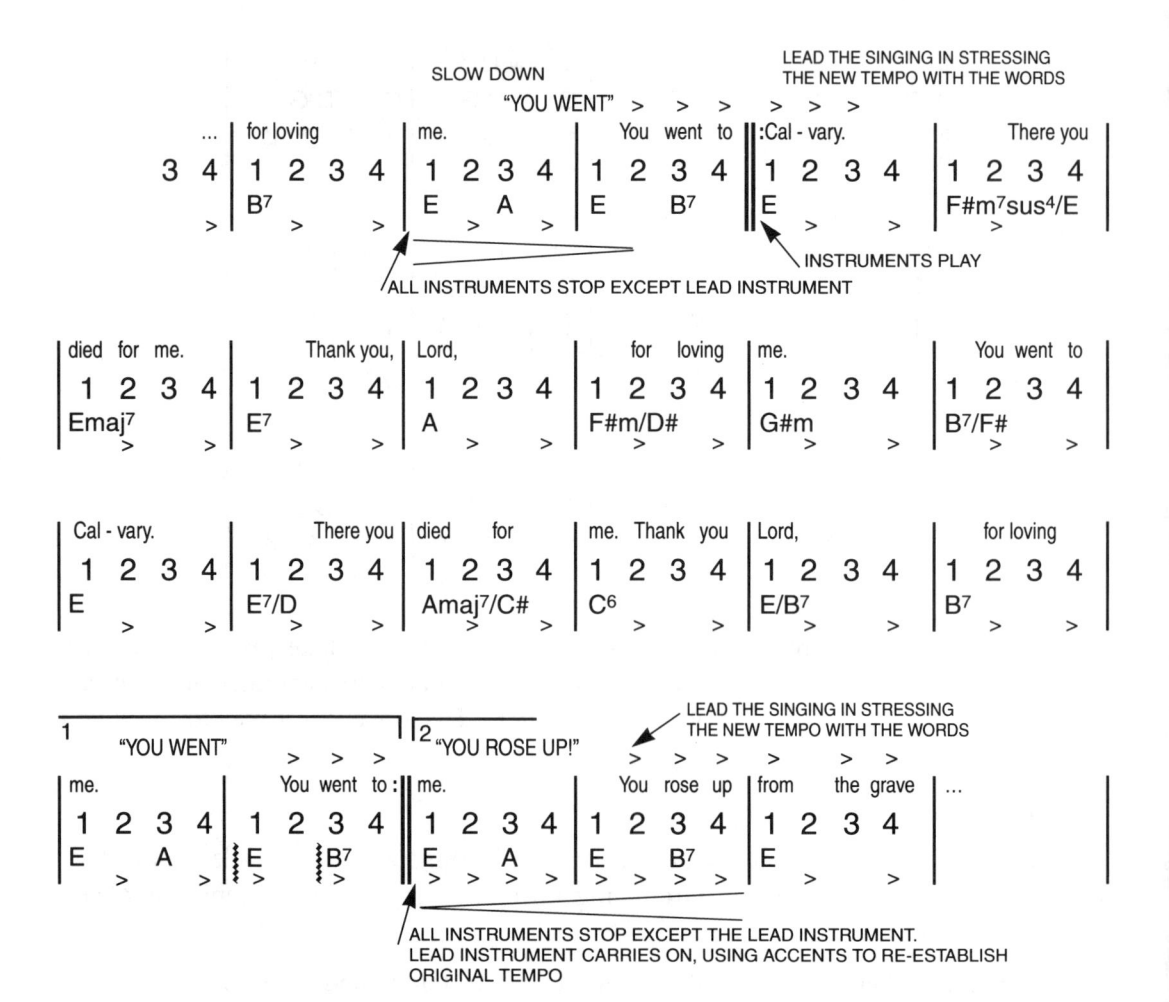

13. At half-tempo then full-tempo

The song *Father, we love You* (SoF 102), works well to two different rhythms.

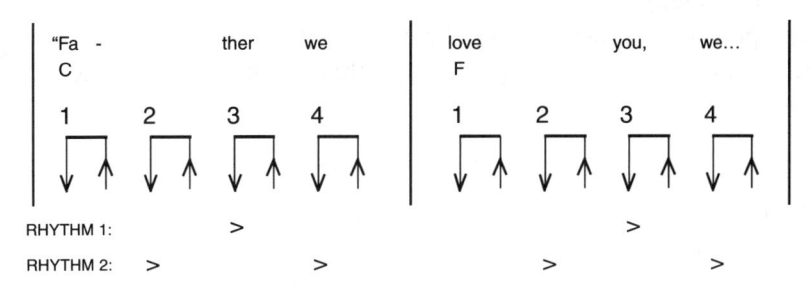

```
"Fa -        ther    we   | love         you,    we...
 C                         |  F
 1      2    3     4       |  1      2    3     4
 ↓↑    ↓↑   ↓↑    ↓↑       |  ↓↑    ↓↑   ↓↑    ↓↑

RHYTHM 1:     >                       >
RHYTHM 2: >        >           >           >
```

The accents in the first rhythm give a more relaxed feel to the song, whereas the second gives a more up-tempo feel to it. Both can be used in the same song with this suggested format:

'Father I love You'; 'Jesus I love you'; 'Spirit I love You' to rhythm 1; then 'Father *we* love You'; 'Jesus *we* love You'; 'Spirit *we* love You' to rhythm 2.

The change in tempo between verse 3 and 4 would have to be well practised, as would the announcement for the change in words to: 'Father *we* love You.'

In the song *Rejoice!* (SoF 480), the choruses could be played with the following rhythm.

```
"Re - ||joice!  Rejoice!  Christ|  is   in   you...
      || 1    2    3    4       |  1    2    3    4        The rhythm of the verses
      || D              G       |  D    G         D        (or one of the verses)
      ||   >       >            |    >         >     etc   could change to:

      ||        "Now is the| time  for  us   to   |...
      || 1    2    3    4  |  1    2    3    4    |
      || A                 |
      ||      >            |            >         |
```

14. Reading Scripture as the congregation hum the tune

A passage of Scripture can almost be given a new dimension when read to musical accompaniment. To enhance the effect even further, you could direct the people to *hum* the tune softly.

(a) Choose a passage of Scripture which matches the mood of the song you've been singing. For example, Psalm 139:13-18 shows how God, in creating each one of us, was expressing something in this universe which couldn't be expressed in any other way. We are a unique message from and about God which no one can duplicate. An ideal song to play before this passage of Scripture is read would be *Jesus, take me as I am* (SoF 305).

(b) Make sure you play softly, otherwise you will swamp both the humming and the reading.

(c) The passage of Scripture must be read slowly and clearly. If you are going to read while playing your guitar, then practise this!

(d) Don't use too lengthy a reading.

(e) At the appropriate place, bring the singing back in. This will mean saying, 'When I feel the touch,' to signal to people that this time through they will be required to sing rather than hum.

15. Singing Scripture to a variation of the song melody

One of the times through a song, instead of reading Scripture, you could sing it.

(a) A good singing voice is required.

(b) The basic melody will have to be altered drastically in order for you to fit the words in.

(c) It is best if the reading begins when the tune begins, otherwise the sung reading will come halfway through the melody. This will sound odd. Therefore, as the previous verse is drawing to a close, pick up your Bible (already open at the passage) and get ready to sing the Scripture as the tune begins.

(d) Practise spontaneously singing Scripture (eg, the Psalms).

16. Reading or singing Scripture at the end of a song

(a) Song (key of G) ends.

(b) You continue to play softly over a chord of G, or play a sequence (a few chords repeated), for example: G(9)–G, Em(9)–Em, C(9)–C, Dsus4–D.

(c) Scripture is read or sung against this backcloth.

You need to be sensitive to the spirit of the passage and complement or emphasise the meaning of the words spoken.

17. Repeating sections of songs

Some songs appear to have two main sections. Having sung the song through a couple of times, instead of singing it a third time, direct people to go back and sing the second section (usually the chorus section).

Note: This will need clear and confident direction.

To illustrate this, here is the end of the second time through the song *I will sing unto the Lord* (SoF 279), with a repeat of the second section:

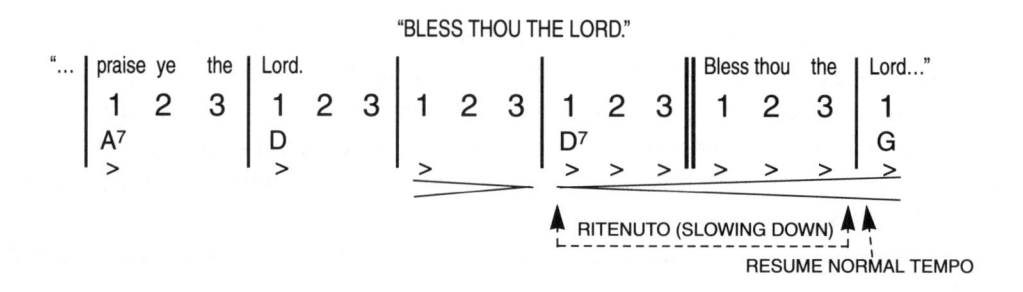

"BLESS THOU THE LORD."

"... praise ye the	Lord.				Bless thou the	Lord..."
1 2 3	1 2 3	1 2 3	1 2 3 ‖ 1 2 3	1
A⁷	D		D⁷		G
>	>	>	> > > ‖ > > >	>

RITENUTO (SLOWING DOWN)
RESUME NORMAL TEMPO

18. Singing only a section of a song

As one song finishes, it may be fitting at times not to sing the whole of another song but just a part of it. For example, imagine the song *Jesus we enthrone You* (SoF 310) has just finished. In the silence that follows you might start singing (with accompaniment or without) the second ('So exalt…') section from the song *Majesty* (SoF 379). (The congregation will hopefully join you.)

19. Linking songs together

Part of the role of a worship leader is to make everything flow as smoothly as possible. Usually when a song finishes, it may be followed by a momentary pause, the title of the next song being announced, a brief comment about this next song, the instrumental introduction setting the tempo of the song and lastly the congregation joining in.

Sometimes the points above don't flow in the way we had hoped. Some possible reasons for this are:

(a) A brief comment, intended as an aid to thoughtful worship, snowballs into a lengthy series of 'blessed thoughts'. This can easily happen if the leader is: (i) nervous, (ii) feeling the people should be responding better, or (iii) insufficiently prepared.

(b) There is an awkward hesitation between the end of the verbal introduction to the next song and your instrumental introduction.

(c) You make a few inspiring comments about the next song, but just as you are about to play the introduction, you realise your capo is not in the correct place. (Make sure capos are changed *as soon as one song finishes and before the verbal introduction to the next song,* otherwise it will take the edge off any illuminating thought-starters.)

One method of overcoming the snags we've been looking at is to link songs together. *Songs of Fellowship* (Music edition) lists the keys of all the songs at the back of the book, so one option is to link songs in the same key.

Tell the congregation what is about to happen. (This isn't necessary in situations where they are used to the idea already.) For instance, you could say something like this: 'We're going to begin our time together by singing the song *I will enter His gates*. Having sung it a number of times, we'll move straight on to sing *For I'm building a people of power.*' (If you say you're going to sing it *a number of times*, then if it feels right, you can carry on for a third time before moving on to the second song.) Make sure your instructions at the beginning are brief, uncomplicated and relaxed.

If they're not, people will have their minds more on getting the format right than on worshipping God.

(a) Announce *very clearly* the title of the new song in the gap between the two songs so that people don't carry on singing the first song.

(b) Drop the volume of the instrument(s) as you make this announcement, otherwise the music may muffle your directions.

(c) Raise the volume of the instrument(s) again afterwards.

(d) Increase the accents on the instrument(s) as you raise the volume.

(e) Sing the first phrase with confidence

Which songs are best linked together? Songs in the same: (a) tempo, (b) key, (c) theme, (d) mood. All four aspects don't *have* to be common to both songs, but at least aim for a few of these characteristics being present.

(a) *Tempo:* We have seen that most songs fall happily into one of seven categories. Each of these groups can be played with one particular strumming pattern. Any two songs from any one of these groups can be joined together, bearing in mind that the songs should be related thematically, to some extent.

(b) *Key:* You may come across two songs which would link together very well thematically, but unfortunately they are not in the same key. Laying aside the issue of key changes between songs, how do we tackle this problem?

Change the key of one or both songs, so that they are both in the same key. For example, the song *Lord, You are more precious* (SoF 368) is in the key of G. The song *I just want to praise You* (SoF 219) is in the key of F (capo 3 in D). The easiest thing to do here is to raise the second song into the key of G, so that both songs are in G. You have to be careful when doing this, keeping in mind the *highest* and *lowest* notes of the melodies of both songs. If you don't take this factor into consideration, people may have to be equipped with special breathing apparatus in order to scale the heights or plumb the depths of these new melodic ranges!

A rough guideline for vocal ranges in songs is (1) Up-tempo songs middle C to E, (2) Slow songs low B to top C (just over one octave).

Whether people are sitting or standing as they sing can also have a bearing on these suggested ranges. You can always get higher when standing.

(c) *Theme:* Don't join two songs together just because they are in the same tempo and key. Ask yourself, 'What do we want to say to God at this point in our worship?' Then ask, 'What songs will express that best?'

(d) *Mood:* Though the songs *For this purpose* (SoF 114) and *Open our eyes, Lord* (SoF 443) are in the same tempo and key, the startling contrast in mood would unsettle any normal flow in worship.

20. Moving back and forth between two songs

Generally speaking, this works best with shorter songs.

1st song ― ― ― >	2nd song ― ― ― >	1st song
(played a number of times)	(played a number of times using variations)	(maybe once only)

The role of leading worship is that of an enabler – helping people to be less aware of themselves and more aware of God. Using songs to create an uninterrupted block time of singing can help to achieve this. The following two examples deal with the mechanics of bridging songs smoothly so that the congregation is not distracted from the purpose of worshipping.

(1) Jesus, Name above all names (SoF 298), *Open our eyes, Lord* (SoF 443). (Capo 4.)

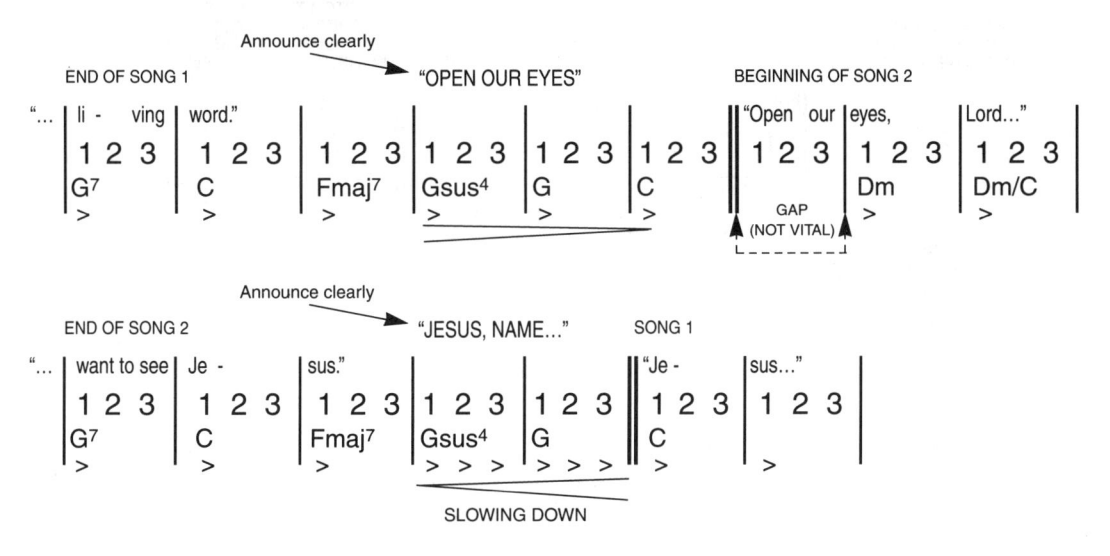

```
                    Announce clearly
 END OF SONG 1       ──► "OPEN OUR EYES"                    BEGINNING OF SONG 2
"... |li-  ving|word."        |          |         |         ||"Open our|eyes,  |Lord..."|
     |1 2 3  |1 2 3 |1 2 3   |1 2 3    |1 2 3    |1 2 3    ||1 2 3   |1 2 3  |1 2 3   |
     |G7     |C     |Fmaj7   |Gsus4    |G        |C        ||        |Dm     |Dm/C    |
     |>      |>     |>       |>        |>        |>        ||  GAP   |>      |>       |
                                                            ▲(NOT VITAL)▲
                                                            └─ ─ ─ ─ ─┘

                    Announce clearly
 END OF SONG 2       ──► "JESUS, NAME..."    SONG 1
"... |want to see|Je- |sus."    |         |         ||"Je-   |sus..." |
     |1 2 3      |1 2 3|1 2 3  |1 2 3    |1 2 3    ||1 2 3  |1 2 3   |
     |G7         |C    |Fmaj7  |Gsus4    |G        ||C      |        |
     |>          |>    |>      |> > >    |> > >    ||>      |>       |
                                SLOWING DOWN
```

Here is a suggested running order of how you might combine these two songs. (*Don't plan it out beforehand*. Let it be a spontaneous response to the people's worship.)

Jesus, Name above all names	– together
Jesus, Name above all names	– Just the ladies (up to 'Emmanuel')
Jesus, Name above all names	– Just the men (from 'Emmanuel')
Open our eyes, Lord	– together
Open our eyes, Lord	– change words: 'Open *my* eyes…'
Open our eyes, Lord	– just the musicians
Jesus, Name above all names	– together (loudly)

Note: Ritenuto (slowing down) could be employed effectively here as you announce that this is the last time through the song.

21. Modulating (changing key) in the same song

This usually involves moving up into a new key. Look at the following example. Having played a few verses of the song in C major, we want to play the next verse in D major. Instead of suddenly leaping from one key to another, we can use either: (a) *one* modulating chord or (b) *two* modulating chords (see bar 3).

103

In my life, Lord (Capo 3 in C, SoF 242).

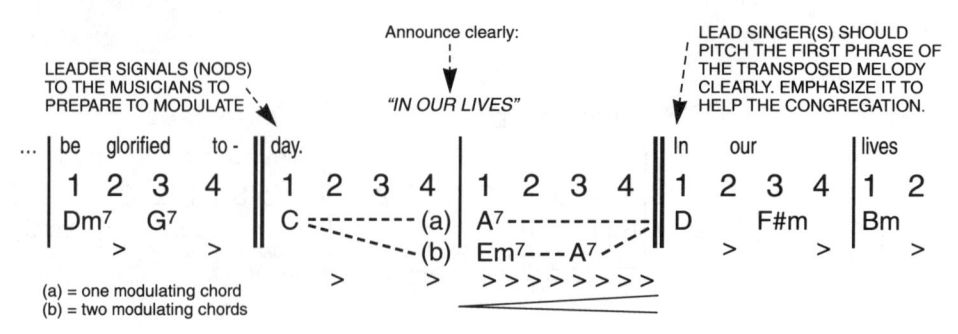

LEADER SIGNALS (NODS) TO THE MUSICIANS TO PREPARE TO MODULATE

Announce clearly: "IN OUR LIVES"

LEAD SINGER(S) SHOULD PITCH THE FIRST PHRASE OF THE TRANSPOSED MELODY CLEARLY. EMPHASIZE IT TO HELP THE CONGREGATION.

... | be glorified to- | day. | | In   our | lives
| 1 2 3 4 | 1 2 3 4 | 1 2 3 4 | 1 2 3 4 | 1 2
| Dm⁷   G⁷ | C ----(a) | A⁷ ---------- | D   F#m | Bm
| >   > | ----(b) | Em⁷---A⁷ | >   > | >
                     | > | > > > > > > > > > |

(a) = one modulating chord
(b) = two modulating chords

Note: (i) Make modulating very clear, raising the volume at this point, and (ii) Take a firm lead in, singing the beginning of the melody in the new key.

(a) Rule for the use of one modulating chord.
This is always the chord on the *5th* note of the scale of the new key – in this example, the key of D major.

(Scale of new key of D)

D   E   F#   G |A| B   C#   D
1   2   3   4 |5| 6   7   8

Modulation chord (A7)

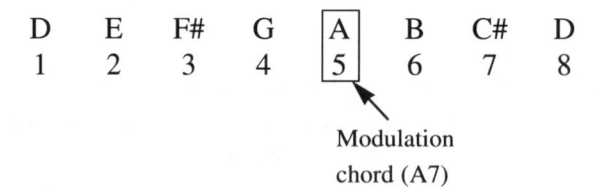

Note: Modulation chords tend to be '7th' chords. In the example above this means that A becomes A7. The addition of a '7th' to the plain chord gives the chord a feeling of incompletion, of being half-way to its goal. It is therefore an ideal chord to use as a 'stepping stone' to a new key.

(b) Rule for the use of two modulating chords.
In conjunction with the chord described in (a) we can use a minor 7th chord on the 2nd note of the scale of the new key.

(Scale of new key of D)

D |E| F#   G |A| B   C#   D
1 |2| 3   4 |5| 6   7   8

Modulation chords (Em7, A7)

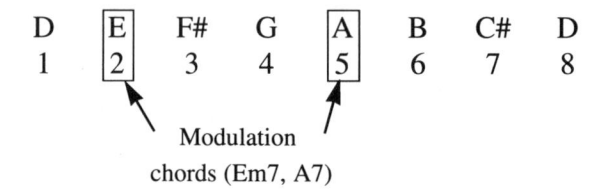

Note: The one-chord modulation (A7) is quite adequate, but the two chords (Em7, A7) sound richer. These last for the same duration as the one chord (in this example, just one bar).

Table of modulations (key changes)

New key (major or minor)		A	B♭	B	C	D♭	D	E♭	E	F	F#	G	A♭
	IIm7	Bm7	Cm7	C#m7	Dm7	E♭m7	Em7	Fm7	F#m7	Gm7	G#m7	Am7	B♭m7
modulation chords	V7	E7	F7	F#7	G7	A♭7	A7	B♭7	B7	C7	C#7	D7	E♭7

How to use the table

Let's imagine you were playing a song in the key of G major. If you wanted to go into the new key of A major, then you would look at the top line for the letter A. The modulation chords necessary to get you into this new key are directly under this letter. In this case, the chords are Bm7 and E7. You could use both these chords or just E7. So your chord progression would look like this:

(a) G → E7 → A; or (b) G → Bm7 → E7 → A

22. Singing counter-melodies (with the same words as the main tune)

Here the basic melody of the song is embroidered with an imitative melody. In order for this to be carried out successfully, one vocalist in the group leading the worship must continue to lead the congregation, while other vocalists (and even instrumentalists) introduce the answering phrase. Consider the following three examples:

(1) *For I'm building a people of power* (SoF 111)

(2) *He is Lord* (SoF 165)

(3) *In my life, Lord* (SoF 242)

[musical notation: "In my life Lord, be glo-ri-fied... / In my life, Lord, be glo-ri-fied..."]

23. *Singing counter-melodies (to 'ooh', 'la', or to new words)*
(a) *'Ooh'*. ('Ooh' often fits better than 'la' in the mood of some songs.)
(b) *New words*. Experiment by making up your own words, either pre-planned or spontaneously.

Emmanuel (SoF 83)

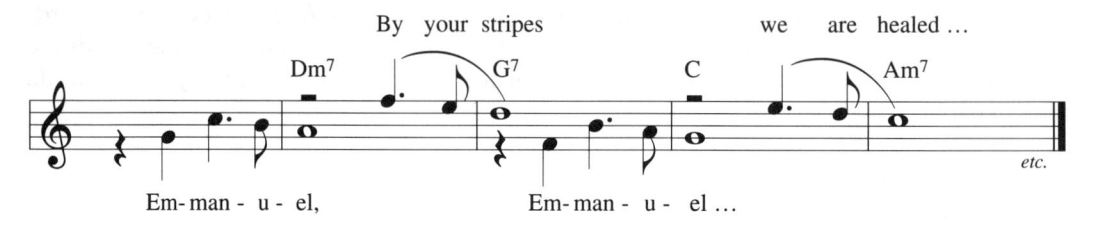

[musical notation: "By your stripes we are healed... / Em-man-u-el, Em-man-u-el..." with chords Dm7, G7, C, Am7]

In the above example I have used a phrase containing three syllables each time. Don't be restricted to such an approach. Your first phrase might be, 'You left Your heavenly throne,' but the second might be, 'My Saviour God.' Try to cultivate a more spontaneous approach.

(c) *'La'*. For example in the song *When the Spirit of the Lord* (SoF 598), after having sung the various verses of this song ('sing', 'clap', 'praise' and 'dance'), direct the congregation to sing the melody to 'la'. After having done this, direct them to return to the original verses by announcing, 'I will *sing*,' etc. (in the gap between the verses). As people come to the chorus section of each verse, you could sing a counter-melody to 'la'.

[musical notation: You sing: la la la la la, la la la la la, la la la la la, la / Congregation: ...I will si——ng, I will si——ng, I will sing as Da-vid sang... with chords Am, Em, B7, Em]

24. *Extended codas (tailpieces)*
The last few bars of a song can be used to act as a framework for improvised worship. So, for example, in the song *Jesus how lovely You are* (SoF 287), you might repeat the

last chorus. Instead of singing the usual tune and words, introduce a new simple melody to 'ah', 'ooh' or 'la'. Most people will at first continue to sing the usual tune or words, but some will follow you and launch out into this uncharted territory. Once some people seem to be picking up that new melody, introduce another. Note, it is *not* important that people follow the correct notes. You are essentially encouraging them to introduce their own vocal expression. As you continue to repeat the eight bars of the chorus, the vocal expression may develop into singing in tongues using fragments of these melodies you are introducing. Here are some suggestions for vocal melodies you might use.

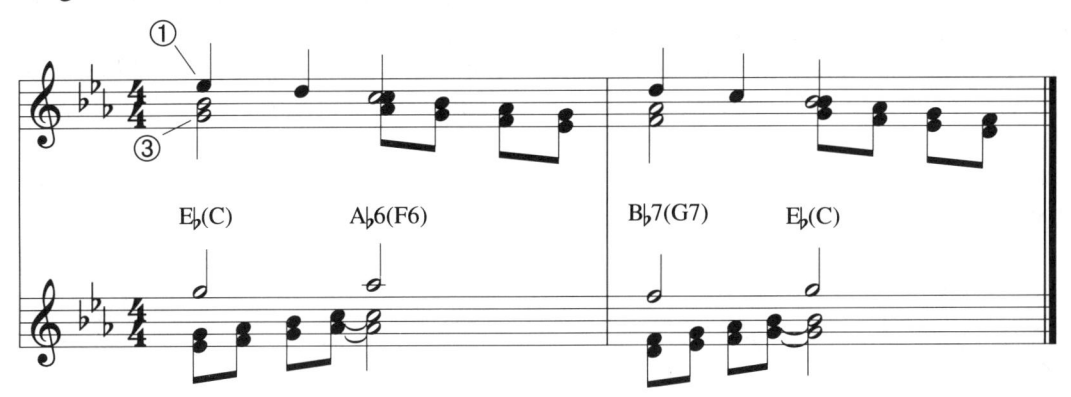

Instead of singing these repeated melodies to 'ah', 'ooh' or 'la' you might find that you are able to fit the words of the song to the melodies with a little adjusting of the melody.

Here is the first melody slightly changed to accommodate the words.

Je - sus, ____ how love-ly You are, ____ You are so gen - tle, so pure and kind ____

Here is the third melody, again slightly altered to fit into the meter of the words.

Je - sus, ____ how love-ly You are, _____ You are so gen - tle, so

25. *Responsive singing*

This was a very common form of singing used in Israel. A phrase would be sung by one or more singers and repeated by others. This was either planned or spontaneous. There are different kinds of responsive singing used in Scripture.

   (a) Leader to another singer (1 Sam 18:7; 21:11; 29:5; Is 6:3-4).
   (b) Leader to a group of singers (Ex 15:21; Ps 44; 47; 99).

(c) One group to another group (Neh 12:31, 40, 42; Ezra 3:11).
(d) Singers to instruments (Is 38:20).
(e) Leader to congregation (Ps 106; 107; 118; 136).

The repetition of an idea was supposed to reinforce it in the mind of the hearer. Listening and participation were both involved. Hence it became a good teaching aid. This can be true today, where leader and congregation sing back and forth around a particular topic (eg, the kindness of God). The main kinds of responses used are (a) imitation, (b) question and answer.

For example, imitative response – leader to congregation. As a song finishes, let it flow into a chord sequence. You then sing a phrase (related to the point you have arrived at in the worship). The congregation echoes this phrase. It is preferable that a gap is left between both phrases, as opposed to them overlapping, as in *I will call upon the Lord* (SoF 266). To help the congregation to join in, you need to say, 'Together,' after singing the phrase first, for them to repeat, before you go on to the next phrase in a similar way.

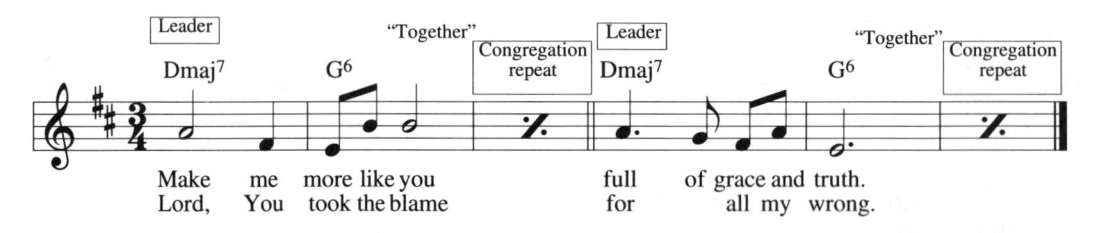

[Musical notation with lyrics:]
Make me more like you, full of grace and truth.
Lord, You took the blame for all my wrong.

If there is a music group or choir, they could regard themselves as a smaller example of the congregation and lead the way strongly with the responsive singing. The congregation should then follow their example. In order that you don't find yourself singing without the response, the music group/choir needs to be quick on the uptake. Any likely misunderstandings should be clarified during rehearsal.

Example:

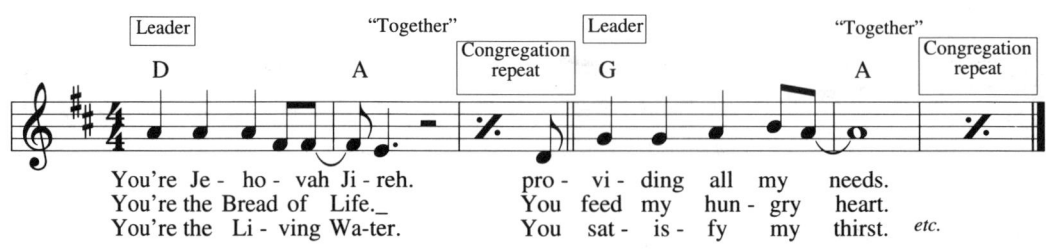

[Musical notation with lyrics:]
You're Je-ho-vah Ji-reh, pro-vi-ding all my needs.
You're the Bread of Life, You feed my hun-gry heart.
You're the Li-ving Wa-ter, You sat-is-fy my thirst. *etc.*

Exercise: Divide singers into groups of two. Give each group a theme, for example, the names of God, warfare, peace, joy, love, the character of God, repentance. Let them have five minutes to prepare how they are going to sing. Each group should be given a chord sequence to sing to as it would become monotonous if only one chord sequence was used for all the groups.

Index of Songs from *Songs of Fellowship* with Pattern Numbers

Authors' titles, where different from first lines, are shown in *italics*.

Pattern number	Key		Song no
3	Bb	Abba, Father	1
2	Eb	Abide with me	2
	E	*Above all others*	372
1	D	Ah Lord God	3
2	G	Alleluia	4
2	C	*Alleluia*	288
7	E	Alleluia! Alleluia!	5
3	F	Alleluia alleluia, give thanks to the risen Lord	6
2	F	All hail King Jesus!	7
2	G	All hail the Lamb	8
7	G/Ab	All hail the power of Jesus' name!	9
2	A	All heaven declares	10
3	Dm	All heaven waits	11
5	C	All over the world	12
2	G	All people that on earth do dwell	13
	C	*All the earth shall worship*	101
2	G	*All the glory*	396
2	D/G	All things bright and beautiful	14
2	A	All you angels round His throne	15
2	D	Almighty God	16
2	Dm	Almighty God, our heavenly Father	17
2	G	Almighty Sovereign Lord	18
3	G	Amazing grace!	19
2	D	*Amazing love*	398
4	G	An army of ordinary people	20
2	G	And can it be?	21
5	D	A new commandment	22
7	G	Angels from the realms of glory	23
2	C	Angel voices ever singing	24
1/7	Em	*Arise, shine*	38
2	E	Arise, shine	78
2	C	A safe stronghold our God is still	25
2	A	Ascribe greatness	26
2	D	As the deer	27
2	G	As we are gathered	28
1	Cm	As we come with praise	29
2	F	As we seek Your face	30
2	A	As with gladness	31
2	C/D	At the name of Jesus	32
1	Dm	At this time of giving	33
2	A	At Your feet we fall	34
1	D	Awake, awake, O Zion	35
2	D	*Awaken Your power*	159
3	F	Away in a manger	36
2	C	*Awesome God*	453
7	G	*Battle hymn*	547
1	F	*Beauty for ashes*	162
5	C	Be bold, be strong	37
1	Em	Behold the darkness	38
2	C	Beneath the cross of Jesus	39
2	D	Be still	40
2	D	Be still and know	41
3	Eb	Be Thou my vision	42
3	F	Bind us together	43
4	C	Blessed assurance	44
2	Em	Blessed be	45
2	C	*Blessed be the Lord God Almighty*	96
2	F	Blessed be the name of the Lord	46

Pattern number	Key		Song no
2	G	Bless the Lord, O my soul	47
2	G	Bless the Lord, O my soul (King of kings)	48
3	G	Blest be the tie	49
2	Eb	Break Thou the Bread of Life	50
3	F	Breathe on me, Breath of God	51
6	Em	Bring a psalm	52
2	E	Broken for me	53
2	Eb	Brother, let me be your servant	54
2	Bb	By Your side	55
3	D	Cause me to come	56
6	G	*Celebrate*	73
6	F	Celebrate Jesus	57
1	Dm	*Celebration song*	244
2	C	Change my heart, O God	58
2/7	C	Christians awake!	59
4	G	Christ is risen	60
7	D	*Christ is risen*	245
2/7	G	Christ the Lord is risen today	61
7	F	Christ triumphant	62
7	D	Clear the road	63
3	D	Colours of day	64
2	E	Come and praise Him, royal priesthood	65
6/7	Bm	Come and praise the living God	66
2	C	Come and see	67
2	F	Come bless the Lord	68
2	Ab	Come into the Holy of Holies	69
6	Bb	Come, let us join our cheerful songs	70
6	G	Come, let us sing	71
3	Eb	Come, let us sing of a wonderful love	72
6	G	Come on and celebrate	73
2	A	Come see the beauty of the Lord	74
1	Cm	*Come with praise*	29
2	G	Come, ye thankful people, come	75
	Dm	*Confession*	17
3	A	Create in me	76
2/7	D	Crown Him with many crowns	77
2/7	E	Darkness like a shroud	78
2	Eb	Dear Lord and Father of mankind	79
2	C	*Do not strive*	325
2	G	Do something new, Lord	80
3	Eb	*Doxology*	462
2	A	Draw me closer	81
2	F	El-Shaddai	82
2	C	Emmanuel	83
2	F	*Emmanuel*	306
2	F	Enter in	84
6	G	Eternal God	85
2	Eb	Exalted, You are exalted	86
2	F	Exalt the Lord our God	87
2	D	Facing a task unfinished	88
2	Cm	*Faithful and just*	371
2	D	Faithful One	89
2	E	*Family song*	169
2	A	Father	90
2	D	Father God, I give all thanks	91
2	Em	Father God I wonder	92
3	D	Father God we worship You	93
2	G	Father, here I am	94

Pattern number	Key		Song no
6	Cm	Father in heaven	95
2	C	Father in heaven how we love You	96
5	F	Father I place into Your hands	97
3	Ab	Father make us one	98
2	G	Father, we adore You	99
2	F	Father, we adore You (Fountain of life)	100
2	C	Father, we adore You, You've drawn us	101
2	C	Father, we love You	102
2	G	Father, You are my portion	103
2	C	Father, Your love is precious	104
6	Am	Fear not	105
4	Em	Fear not, rejoice and be glad	106
7	D	Fight the good fight	107
2	D/F	Fill Thou my life, O Lord my God	108
2	C	*Fire of God*	342
2/6	G	For all the saints	109
	F	*For evermore*	603
3	F	For His name is exalted	110
1	C	For I'm building a people of power	111
6	Bb	For the beauty of the earth	112
7	Cm	For the Lord is marching on	113
4	D	For this purpose	114
2	F	For Thou O Lord art high	115
3	Bb	For unto us a child is born	116
2	E	For we see Jesus	117
4	D	*For Your kingdom*	382
2	Bb	For Your wonderful deeds	118
2	F	*Fountain of life*	100
4	Eb	Freely, freely	129
	D	From all that dwell below the skies	119
2	Eb	From heaven You came	120
5	Eb	From the rising of the sun	121
4	D	From the sun's rising	122
2	A	*Give Him praise*	15
2	F	Give me life, Holy Spirit	123
2/6	D	Give thanks	124
6	C	Give thanks to the Lord	125
2	C	Glorious Father	126
7	Eb	Glorious things of Thee are spoken	127
6	G	Glory	128
2	E	*Glory and praise*	616
6	D	*Glory to the Lord*	501
2	F	*Go*	211
3	Eb	God forgave my sin	129
1/7	Em	God has exalted Him	130
6	C	God has spoken to His people	131
7	Gm	God is good	132
2	Em	God is here, God is present	133
5	G	God is our Father	134
2	F	God is working His purpose out	135
2	G	God of all comfort	136
2	D	God of glory	137
2	Am	God of grace	138
2	G	God of grace and God of glory	139
2	C	*God with us*	172
7	D	Go forth	486
3	F	Good Christian men rejoice	140
6	Em	Great and marvellous	141
6	G	Great and marvellous are Thy works	142
1	Em	Great and wonderful	143
2	D	*Great are Your works*	638
5	A	Great is the Lord and greatly to be praised	144
2	G	Great is the Lord and most worthy	

109

Pattern number	Key	Title	Song no
		of praise	145
1	Cm	Great is the Lord and mighty in power	146
3	D	Great is Thy faithfulness	147
2	G	Guide me, O Thou great Jehovah	148
7	C	Hail, Thou once despised Jesus	149
2	G	Hail to the Lord's Anointed	150
1	F	Hallelujah, for the Lord our God	151
2	E	Hallelujah, my Father	152
1	F	*Hallelujah ... our God reigns*	*151*
2	F	Hallelujah! sing to Jesus	153
7	G	Hark the glad sound	154
2	F	Hark! the herald angels sing	155
2	F	Have Thine own way, Lord	156
3	G	Healing grace	157
2	E	*Heal our nation*	*365*
2	D	Hear, O Lord our cry	158
2	D	Hear, O Shepherd	159
2/6	G	*Heaven is in my heart*	*416*
3	A	Heavenly Father, I appreciate You	160
1	Em	*Hebrew names for God*	*283*
6	G	He came to earth	161
5	F	He gave me beauty	162
2	C	He holds the key	163
4	G	He is exalted	164
2	G	He is Lord	165
2	E	He is our peace	166
2	E	Here I am	167
3	Ab	Here is love	168
6	E	Here we are	169
2	E	He shall reign	170
1	D	He that is in us	171
6	C	He walked where I walk	172
2	D	He was pierced	173
6	Eb	He who would valiant be	174
6	F	Higher, higher	175
2	Eb	*Higher than the heavens*	*622*
2	Cm	*His body was broken*	*490*
2	D	His name is higher	176
3	F	His name is Wonderful	177
6	D	*History makers*	*259*
	F	His voice like the sea	178
2	G	Hold me, Lord	179
2	G	Holiness unto the Lord	180
2	G	*Holy and anointed One*	*293*
2	Eb	*Holy ground*	*569*
2	G	Holy, holy, holy	181
3	G	Holy, holy, holy is the Lord	182
2	D/Eb	Holy, holy, holy, Lord God Almighty!	183
2	F	Holy, holy, holy Lord	184
2	Em	Holy is the Lord	185
2	F	Holy One	186
2	C	*Holy Spirit, come*	*343*
2	D	Holy Spirit, lead me to my Father	187
2	C	Holy Spirit, we welcome You	188
6/7	G	Hosanna	189
2	F	*Hosanna to the son of David*	*627*
2	A	How great Thou art	425
2	G	How I love You	190
2	D	How lovely is Thy dwelling place	191
5	Bb	How lovely on the mountains	192
6	Eb	How precious, O Lord	193
2	D	How sweet the name of Jesus sounds	194
2	F	How You bless our lives	195
2	E	I am a lighthouse	196
6	Eb	I am a new creation	197
2	F	I am a wounded soldier	198
2	F	I am not ashamed	199
7	Bb	I am the Bread of Life	200
2	E	I am the God that healeth thee	201
3	G	I am trusting Thee, Lord Jesus	202
2	E	I believe in Jesus	203
2	D	I can almost see	204
2	C	I cannot tell	205
5	F	I delight greatly in the Lord	206

Pattern number	Key	Title	Song no
2	F	*I exalt Thee*	*115*
2	A	I exalt You	207
5	D	If I were a butterfly	208
6	A	I get so excited, Lord	209
2	G	I give You all the honour	210
2	F	I give You now	211
6	G	I have a destiny	212
2	D	I have found	213
2	C	I have made a covenant	214
2	Gm/Em	I heard the voice of Jesus say	215
1	D	I hear the sound of rustling	216
2	G	I hear the sound of the army of the Lord	217
2	F	I just want to praise You	218
2	E	I just want to praise You (Lord, I lift you high)	219
6	D	I know not why God's wondrous grace	220
2	C	I lift my eyes up	221
2	D	I lift my hands (Most of all)	222
2	E	I lift my hands (I will serve no foreign god)	223
2	C	I lift my voice	224
3	A	I live	225
2	F	I love You, Lord	226
2	Ab	I love You, my Lord	227
2	F	I love You with the love of the Lord	228
2	E	I'm accepted	229
2	A	*I'm for ever grateful*	*631*
6	A	*I'm forgiven*	*209*
6	C	I'm gonna thank the Lord	230
3	D	I'm in love with You	231
2	D	Immanuel	232
2	D	Immanuel, O Immanuel	233
3	G	Immortal, invisible	234
6	D	I'm not alone	235
2	D	I'm special	236
6	Em	In heavenly armour	237
3	D	In heavenly love abiding	238
6	D	In Him we live and move	239
2	D	In majesty He comes	240
3	D	In moments like these	241
2	D	*In my generation*	*260*
2	Eb	In my life, Lord	242
2	F	In the bleak midwinter	243
1	Dm	In the presence of Your people	244
7	D	In the tomb so cold	245
4	Em	In through the veil	246
1	Dm	In Thy presence	247
2	G	I really want to worship You my Lord	633
3	D	I receive Your love	248
2	G	*Isaiah 6*	*181*
2	G	I see the Lord	249
2	A	Isn't He beautiful?	250
2	Am	*I stand complete in You*	*138*
2	A	*I stand in awe*	*621*
2	F	It came upon the midnight clear	251
3	D	It is a thing most wonderful	252
6	G	It is good for me	253
5	G	It is no longer I that liveth	254
5	F	It's a happy day	255
2	G	It's the presence of Your Spirit, Lord, we need	256
	Bb	It's Your blood	257
2	G	I wanna sing	258
2	D	I want to be a history maker	259
2	D	I want to serve the purpose of God	260
4	D	I want to walk with Jesus Christ	261
2	G	I was made to praise You	262
6	G	I was once in darkness	263
7	G	I will build My church	264
2	D	I will call	265
1	D	I will call upon the Lord	266
3	G	I will change your name	267
1	Eb	I will enter His gates	268
2	Bb	I will give thanks to Thee	269
2	D	I will give You praise	270

Pattern number	Key	Title	Song no
6	Bb	I will magnify	271
2	G	I will praise You all my life	272
5	D	I will rejoice in You and be glad	273
7	Gm	I will rejoice, I will rejoice	274
6	F	I will rise and bless You, Lord	275
2	F	I will seek Your face, O Lord	276
2	E	*I will serve no foreign god*	*223*
6	D	I will sing of the mercies	277
3	F	I will sing the wondrous story	278
4	D	I will sing unto the Lord	279
	Em	*I will sing Your praises*	*92*
2	E	I will speak out	280
/7		I will worship You, Lord	281
2	G	*I worship You*	*210*
2	G	I worship You, Almighty God	282
/7	Em	*Jehovah Jireh*	*283*
/7	Em	Jehovah Jireh, my Provider	284
7	C	Jesus Christ is risen today	285
6	F	Jesus has sat down	286
2	E	Jesus, how lovely You are	287
2	C	Jesus, I love You	288
2	E	Jesus is King	289
2	F	*Jesus is Lord*	*178*
3	Ab	Jesus is Lord!	290
2	C	Jesus is Lord of all	291
7	E	*Jesus is our King*	*5*
2	F	Jesus, I worship You	292
2	G	Jesus, Jesus	293
2	Bb	Jesus, Jesus, Jesus	294
2	D	Jesus, King of kings	295
7	Bb	Jesus lives	296
/7	Em	Jesus, lover of my soul	297
3/4	D	Jesus, Name above all names	298
	Dm	Jesus put this song into our hearts	299
3	A	Jesus, send more labourers	300
2	F/C	Jesus shall reign	301
2	Bb	Jesus shall take the highest honour	302
	Eb	Jesus, stand among us	303
2	G/D	Jesus, stand among us in Thy risen power	304
2	E	Jesus take me as I am	305
2	D	Jesus, the Name above all names	306
7	D	Jesus! the name high over all	307
3	G	Jesus, the very thought of Thee	308
6	G	Jesus, we celebrate Your victory	309
2	A	Jesus, we enthrone You	310
2	Eb	Jesus, You are changing me	311
3	F	Jesus, You are the radiance	312
2	G	Join all the glorious names	313
2	C	*Join our hearts*	*363*
2/7	D	Joy to the world	314
1	Dm	*Jubilate Deo*	*315*
1	Dm	Jubilate, everybody	315
3	Eb/D	Just as I am	316
3	C	Just like You promised	317
2	G	King for ever	318
2	G	*King of kings*	*48*
2	G	*King of kings*	*161*
7	A	King of kings	319
6	G	*King of saints*	*142*
2	Bb	Lamb of God	320
2/7	E	Lead us, heavenly Father, lead us	321
2	G	Led like a lamb	322
2	G	*Let forgiveness flow*	*94*
7	D	Let God arise	323
2	G	Let God speak	324
2	C	Let Me have My way among you	325
2	D	Let our praise to You be as incense	326
6	G	Let praises ring	327
7	F	*Let the flame burn brighter*	*583*
5	F	Let there be glory and honour	328
3	F	Let there be love	329
2	E	Let us break bread together	330
6	E	Let us go to the house of the Lord	331
6	A	Let us praise His name with dancing	332
7	Bb	Let us with a gladsome sound	333
6	Em	*Let Your kingdom come*	*367*

Pattern number	Key	Song	Song no
7	D	Let Your living water flow	334
7	C	Lift high the cross	335
2	Ab	Lift up your heads to the coming King	336
2/7	A	Lift up your heads, O you gates	337
2/7	A	Lift up your heads, O ye gates	338
6	G	Light a flame	339
2	D	Lighten our darkness	340
7	A	Light has dawned	341
2	C	Light of the world	342
3	D	Light up the fire	64
2	C	Like a gentle breeze	343
2	D	Like a Lamb	173
2/7	C	Like a river glorious	344
7	C	Lion of Judah	345
2	F	Living sacrifice	508
2	G	Living under the shadow of His wing	346
2/7	G	Lo, He comes with clouds descending	347
5	G	Look and see the glory of the King	348
2/7	Gb	Look, ye saints, the sight is glorious	349
2	G	Lord and Father, King for ever	350
2	Eb	Lord, be glorified	242
2	G	Lord, come and heal Your church	351
2	Bb	Lord, enthroned in heavenly splendour	352
2	E	Lord God, heavenly King	353
2	E	Lord, have mercy	354
6	A	Lord, how majestic You are	355
2	E	Lord, I lift You high	219
2	G	Lord, I will celebrate Your love	356
2	D	Lord Jesus Christ	357
2	G	Lord Jesus here I stand	358
2	A	Lord, keep my heart tender	359
3	F	Lord make me an instrument	360
6	G	Lord of lords	361
6	A	Lord, the light of Your love	362
2	C	Lord we come	363
2	G	Lord we give You praise	364
2	E	Lord we long for You	365
2	A	Lord, we worship You	366
6	Em	Lord, You are calling	367
2	G	Lord, You are more precious	368
2	A	Lord, You are so precious to me	369
6	G	Lord, You put a tongue in my mouth	370
2	Cm	Lord, You're faithful and just	371
2	E	Lord, Your glory fills my heart	372
2	Em	Lord, Your name is holy	373
6	G	Lord, Your name is wonderful	374
4	G	Love beyond measure	375
2	F	Love came down at Christmas	376
3	G	Love divine	377
2	Bb	Low in the grave He lay	378
2	G	Majesty	379
6	A	Make a joyful melody	380
2	D	Make me a channel of your peace	381
2	D	Make me a dreamer	382
2	G	Make us one, Lord	383
7	G	Make way	384
2	F	Man of Sorrows	385
2	F	Master speak! Thy servant heareth	386
2	C	May my life	387
2	D	May the fragrance	388
2/7	Bb	May we be a shining light	389
3	C	Meekness and majesty	390
2	D	Mighty God	391
2	Gm	More love, more power	392
4	C	Morning has broken	393
2 of all		Most of all	222
2	G	Move Holy Spirit	394
2	G	My delight	103
7	G	My God, how wonderful Thou art	395
2	C	My heart is full	396
5/6	G	My Lord, He is the fairest of the fair	397

Pattern number	Key	Song	Song no
2	D	My Lord, what love is this	398
3/4	C	My peace	399
2	D	My song is love unknown	400
2	G	My soul longs for You	401
2	G	No one but You Lord	402
6	E	Not unto us	403
6/7	D	Not without a cause	404
2/7	Eb	Now thank we all our God	405
2	D	Now unto the King	406
7	D	O Breath of Life, come sweeping through us	407
7	G	O come all ye faithful	408
2	G	O come let us adore Him	409
2	Em	O come O come Emmanuel	410
2	G	O faithful God	272
2	Eb/D	O for a heart to praise my God	411
7	G	O for a thousand tongues	412
6	D	O give thanks	413
1/7	Bm	O give thanks	536
2	D	O God my Creator	414
2/7	C	O God, our help in ages past	415
6	G	O, heaven is in my heart	416
2	Bb	O I love You, Lord	522
5	F	O I will sing unto You with joy	417
2	E/D	O Jesus, I have promised	418
2	D	O let the Son of God enfold you	419
6	F	O little town of Bethlehem	420
2	G	O Lord, give me an undivided heart	421
2	C	O Lord, have mercy on me	422
2	Em	O Lord, hear my prayer	423
2	D	O Lord most Holy God	424
2	A	O Lord my God!	425
2	G	O Lord our God	426
2	E	O Lord our God, You are a great God	427
1/7	Em	O Lord, our Lord	428
2	C	O Lord, the clouds are gathering	429
2	D	O Lord, You are my God	430
6	Gm	O Lord, You are my light	431
2	F	O Lord, You're beautiful	432
2	C	O Lord, Your tenderness	433
2	G	O love that wilt not let me go	434
6	D	O magnify the Lord	435
2	A	O my Lord, You are most glorious	436
2	F	O my Saviour, lifted	437
2/7	F	Once in royal David's city	438
1	Em	One shall taste another	439
2	G	One thing I ask	440
2/6	C	Only by grace	441
2	G	Only You	402
7	Eb	Onward, Christian soldiers	442
3	D	Open our eyes, Lord	443
2	C	Open your eyes	444
3	F	O praise ye the Lord	445
2	C	O sacred head once wounded	446
6	F	O taste and see	447
2	F	O that You would bless me	448
2	Bb	On the joy of Your forgiveness	449
4	F	O the valleys shall ring	450
3	Eb/G	O Thou who camest from above	451
	D	Our confidence is in the Lord	452
2	C	Our God is an awesome God	453
5	Bb	Our God reigns	192
2	D	Out of Your great love	454
6	G	O, we are more than conquerors	455
3	G	O worship the King	456
3	D	O worship the Lord	457
2	A	O you gates	337
2	Eb	Peace is flowing like a river	458
2	F	Peace like a river	459
4	A	Peace to you	460
2	Gm	Praise God for the body	461
3	Eb	Praise God from whom all blessings flow	462
2	E	Praise Him	463
5	E	Praise Him on the trumpet	464

Pattern number	Key	Song	Song no
4	G	Praise Him, Praise Him! Jesus our blessèd Redeemer	465
2	D	Praise, my soul, the King of heaven	466
2	D	Praise song	507
6	G	Praise the Lord	467
2	Eb	Praise the name of Jesus	468
3	G	Praise to the Holiest in the height	469
3	F	Praise to the Lord, the Almighty	470
3	G	Praise ye the Lord	471
2	Eb	Praise You, Lord	472
6	C	Prepare the way	473
7/2	D	Prepare the way	63
2	C	Prince of Peace You are	474
2	C	Psalm 121	221
2	E	Psalm 122	331
6	D	Psalm 34	435
2	E	Purify my heart	475
7	C	Raise up an army	476
6	F	Reconciled	477
2	E	Refiner's fire	475
2	G	Reign in me	478
2	Dm	Reigning in all splendour	479
6	D	Rejoice	480
6	D	Rejoice, rejoice, rejoice!	481
2	C	Rejoice, the Lord is King!	482
2	D	Restore, O Lord	483
6	G	Revival	484
2	D	Revive us again	158
2/7	Bb	Ride on, ride on in majesty	485
2	D	Rise up	486
3	Eb	River wash over me	487
2/7	Eb/Bb	Rock of ages	488
5	F	Rock of my salvation	417
2	F	Sacrificial love	387
2	G	See amid the winter's snow	489
2	Cm	See Him come	490
2	D	See Him lying on a bed of straw	491
2	G	See His glory	492
2	Eb	Seek ye first	493
3	G	Set my spirit free	494
6	A	Shine, Jesus, shine	362
6	D	Shout for joy	495
1	G	Shout for joy and sing	496
6	A	Show Your power, O Lord	497
3	Bb	Silent night	498
2	Cm	Sing Hellelujah to the Lord	499
6	A	Sing praises unto God	500
6	Bb	Sing to the Lord	501
6	G	Sing unto the Lord a new song	502
2	A	So freely	503
2	D	Soften my heart	504
3	D	Soften my heart, Lord	505
2	F/G	Soldiers of Christ, arise	506
2/7	Bb	Song for the nations	389
2	D	Son of God	507
2	F	Sovereign Lord	508
2	A	Spirit breathe on us	509
2	D	Spirit of God	204
2	F	Spirit of the living God (Daniel Iverson)	510
2	C	Spirit of the living God (Paul Armstrong)	511
2	D	Spirit Song	419
2/6	D/G	Stand up, and bless the Lord	512
7	A	Stand up, stand up for Jesus	513
2	G	Stretch out Your hand	18
2/6	E	Such love, pure as the whitest snow	514
2	G	Such love, such grace	515
6	G	Sweet fellowship	516
2	G	Swing wide the gates	517
3	C	Take eat, this is My body	518
3	F	Take my life, and let it be	519
2	D/F	Tell out, my soul	520
2	G	Thanks be to God	521
2	Bb	Thank You for the cross	522

111

Pattern number	Key	Title	Song no
5	G	Thank You, Jesus	523
1	F	Thank You, Lord, for this fine day	524
6	Em	The battle belongs to the Lord	237
5	D	*The butterfly song*	*208*
6/7	Em	*The church invincible*	*570*
2	D	The church's one foundation	525
	G	The church's one foundation (Dave Bilbrough)	526
3	G	The day Thou gavest, Lord, is ended	527
4	D	The earth is the Lord's	528
6	G	*The feast is ready*	*550*
3	D	*The first nowell*	*529*
1	Dm	*The giving song*	*33*
2/6	Em	The God of Abraham praise	530
2	G	The head that once was crowned with thorns	531
4	E	The King is among us	532
2/7	A	*The King of glory*	*338*
7	A	*The King of glory comes*	*319*
6	G/D	The King of love	533
7	F	The Lord has given	534
1	D	The Lord handed forth	535
1	Bm	The Lord is marching out	536
3	F	The Lord's my Shepherd	537
6		The Lord your God is in your midst	538
2	E	The nations are waiting	539
2	C	The price is paid	540
5	Bb	Therefore the redeemed	541
2	Eb	There is a green hill far away	542
3	G	There is a name I love to hear	543
2	E	There is a Redeemer	544
6	D	There is power in the name of Jesus	545
2	F	There's a quiet understanding	546
6	G	There's a sound in the wind	547
2	Eb	*The Servant King*	*120*
2	Eb	*The servant song*	*54*
2	Bb	The Spirit of the Lord	548
2	F	The steadfast love of the Lord	549
1/7	Em	*The trees of the field*	*640*
6	G	The trumpets sound	550
1	Em	*The wine of the kingdom*	*439*
6	D	Thine be the glory	551
2	G	Thine, O Lord, is the greatness	552
1	E	This is the day	553
3	C	*This is your God*	*390*
3	Bb	Thou art worthy	554
2	F	Thou didst leave Thy throne	555
2	D	Thou, O Lord, art a shield about me	556
3	G	Thou, whose almighty word	557
7	Cm	Through our God	558
3	G	To God be the glory!	559

Pattern number	Key	Title	Song no
2	C	To Him who sits on the throne	560
2	G	*To seek Your face*	*136*
3	F	Trust and obey	599
2	G	*Undivided heart*	*421*
6	F	Unto Thee, O Lord	561
3	D	*Unto the King*	*406*
6	G	Unto You, O Lord	562
3	G	*Victory song*	*559*
6	G	We are a chosen people	563
5	G	We are all together	564
6	C	We are a people of power	565
2	Eb	We are being built into a temple	566
2	E	We are here to praise You	567
7	D	We are in God's army	568
2	F	*We are more than conquerors*	*581*
2	Eb	We are standing	569
7	Em	We are the hands of God	570
2	F	We are Your people	571
7	F#m	*We believe*	*572*
2	Eb	We break this bread	573
7	Eb	We bring the sacrifice of praise	574
7	D	We declare that the kingdom of God is here	575
2	E	We declare there's only one Lord	576
2	G	We declare Your majesty	577
2	C	*We exalt Your name*	
2	G	We extol You	578
2	Eb	*We have come into His house*	
2	Eb	We have come into this place	579
6	F	We have come to Mount Zion	580
2	F	We know that all things	581
6	E	We'll sing a new song	582
2	F	We'll walk the land	583
6	G	We place You on the highest place	584
2	A	We plough the fields and scatter	585
6	D	We really want to thank You, Lord	586
2	F	We rest on Thee, our Shield and our Defender!	587
3	C	We shall be as one	588
2	D	*We shall rise*	*240*
6	F	We shall stand	589
6	Cm	*We will crown Him*	*95*
3	Eb	We will glorify	590
2	C	We will honour You	591
6	G	*We will magnify*	*426*
2	C	*We worship at Your feet*	*67*
2	Em	We worship and adore You	592
5	G	*We welcome You*	*564*
2	F	What a friend we have in Jesus	593
2	D	When I feel the touch	594
2	C	When I look into Your holiness	595
3	D	When I survey the wondrous cross	596

Pattern number	Key	Title	Song no
6	Bb	When morning gilds the skies	597
1/7	Em	When the Spirit of the Lord	598
3/4	F	When we walk with the Lord	599
3	Eb	Where you go I will go	600
6	E	Whether you're one	601
2	F	While shepherds watched	602
	F	Who can ever say they understand	603
2	Bb	Who can sound the depths of sorrow	604
3	A	Who is He in yonder stall?	605
3	F	Who is like unto Thee?	606
7	C	Who is on the Lord's side?	607
2/7	Eb	*Who is this?*	*608*
6	F	Wind, wind, blow on me	609
2/6	G	With all my heart	610
6	C	With my whole heart	611
2	C	*Worthy is the Lamb*	*636*
2	A	Wonderful love	612
2	D	Worship the Lord	613
3	D	Worthy art Thou	614
2/6	G	Worthy is the Lamb seated on the throne	615
2	E	Worthy is the Lamb who was slain	616
6	Eb	Worthy, O worthy are You Lord	617
6	G	Worthy, the Lord is worthy	618
6/7	C	Ye holy angels bright	619
3	Bb	Ye servants of God	620
2	A	You are beautiful	621
2	Eb	You are compassionate	622
6	G	You are crowned with many crowns	623
2	D	You are here	624
4	A	*You are my everything*	*355*
2	Dm	You are my hiding place	625
2	C	You are the Holy One	626
2	F	You are the King of Glory	627
2	Eb	You are the mighty King	628
2	G	You are the Vine	629
2	G	*You are the One*	*190*
2	G	You are worthy	630
2	A	You did not wait for me	631
3	G	You have been given	632
2	G	You laid aside Your majesty	633
6	G	You make my heart feel glad	634
2	G	You, O Lord	635
2/7	C	You purchased men	636
2	C	*You're alive*	*322*
2	F	*Your love overwhelms me*	*104*
2	D	Your mercy flows	637
2	D	Your works, Lord	638
7	C	You sat down	639
1/7	Em	You shall go out with joy	640